To Freedom

Contents

Introduction 1
   Why Python? 2
   For whom is this book written? 2
   Signs in the book 2
   Final Note 2
Chapter 1 3
   Basics 3
      Numeric data type 3
      Strings 3
      List 4
      Set 5
      Tuple 5
      Dictionary 5
      Lists and dictionaries 5
      Dictionaries 9
      If and condition 12
      Loops and functions 14
      Function 16
      lambda 17
      Class 18
      Exception/ error handling 19
      Exception 20
      Handling exception 21
      Opening/closing files 21
   Mixed Examples 24
   Mini project: Random walk 25

Chapter 2 30
Numpy 30
Creating arrays 30
Indexing 33
Properties 36
Combining or splitting 37
Basic math 38
Math (intermediate) 40
Import and export 43
Mini project 44

Chapter 3 45
Pandas 45
Creating DataFrames 45
Loading the database 47
Drop method 49
Columns to drop 51
Rows to drop 51
Date and time 52
Relocation of columns 53
Subsets 54
Summarize data 55
New columns 57
Filtering a DataFrame 59
Sorting 60
Groupby 61
Mini project 62

Chapter 4 66
Matplotlib 66
Creating a figure and a set of subplots 66

- Plotting y versus x as lines and/or markers 66
- Setting the title 67
- Setting x and y axis label 67
- Generating the legend 67
- Saving the graph in the desired format 67
- Example 1 68
- Example2 69
- Example3 71
- Example4 74
- Example5 76
- Example6 78
- Example7 80

Chapter 5 83
- Scipy 83
  - Derivative 83
  - Integration 84
  - Interpolation 85
  - Curve fitting 89
  - Root finding 90
  - Differential Equation 91
  - Linear Algebra 94
- Mini project 97

Chapter 6 102
- Fourier series 102

Chapter 7 111
- Single degree of freedom system 111
  - Example1: 115
  - Example2: 116

Chapter8 120

    Concrete bean design 120
    Elastic design 121
    Elasto-plastic design 123
Chapter9 129
    Finite element method for beams 129
        Example1 129
        Example2 137
Appendix 1 141
    Install python 141
    Install libraries 142
    Install vscode 143
        Virtual environment 143
Appendix2 148
    Markers for Matplotlib 148
    Line styles for Matplotlib 148
    Basic Colors for Matplotlib 148

Introduction

Nowadays, acquiring proficiency in a programming language is necessary for students and experts who are engaged in activities such as simulations, analysis, and design.

The year 2023 has marked a significant milestone in the widespread adoption of artificial intelligence for commercial purposes. With the introduction of chat-GPT, OpenAI opened a big window of opportunities, enabling individuals, including those who are not considered Tech-Savvy, to use the power of AI across a vast variety of subjects ranging from language learning to enhancing professional writing.

These developments are of great significance to engineers, as they need to stay updated with the advancements to effectively utilize existing machine learning algorithms and develop customized optimization techniques.

This book aims to provide readers with the fundamentals of Python language, coupled with highly useful open-source libraries. We hope this book makes a small contribution to the Civil Engineering Society and somehow bridges the gap between engineering Concepts and programming.

For this purpose: chapter 1 discusses Python's elementary rules and syntaxes.

Chapter 2 shows how Numpy could empower scientists to conduct numerical operations quickly and accurately.

Chapter 3 highlights the necessity of pandas making it easier for users to store, manage and manipulate data.

Chapter 4 depicts how graphs are drawn which could be very conducive for visualizing data and information.

Chapter 5 discusses basic methods of a powerful library entitled Scipy which basically was developed to operate advanced scientific tasks. With Scipy, readers will discover how to perform advanced data manipulation tasks.

Chapters 6 to 9 contain four projects with detailed explanations. These projects have different levels starting from beginner to upper intermediate.

- Chapter6: Fourier series (beginner)
- Chapter7: Single-degree freedom problem (intermediate)
- Chapter8: Simple design of concrete beams (intermediate)
- Chapter9: Finite element method for beam (upper intermediate)

There are also two appendices that include installation instructions and information on matplotlib styles.

Why Python?

Python stands out as one of the top choices for coding due to some of its compelling qualities. Firstly, it is super easy to learn as it is remarkably similar to human language. Secondly, a plethora of resources, including written tutorials and video clips have been prepared that compel starters to embark on their journey with Python. Finally, everyday useful libraries are published in addition to popular libraries that already exist, which target difficulties in programming. For instance, TensorFlow is a well-known framework for deep learning and every update improves the efficacy of programming within the framework.

For whom is this book written?
- Every civil engineering student who aspires to start coding.
- Every enthusiast with literacy in civil engineering basic concepts and practices.

Signs in the book
- Throughout the book all codes are displayed after **In** followed by **Out** as the outcome of the code.
- All Python syntaxes are written in `this format`.
- Explanations of the codes may accompany **NB**, emphasizing an important point.

Final Note

If you have any comments, please do not hesitate to contact us. Our team highly values your points of view and incorporates constructive feedback into our subsequent revisions.

Chapter 1

Chapter 1

Basics

This chapter provides a brief explanation of the basics, and instead of engaging the reader in frustrating theories, this book aims to illuminate the concepts with various examples.

Numeric data type

Three classes for numbers exist in Python as following:

Class integer: this class contains whole numbers like: -10, 10, 0, 1, -2. `int()`

Class float: this class represents real numbers like 0.5, -0.002. `float()`

Class complex: this class is made up of two parts, first: the real part. Second: the imaginary part. For example: 5+8j

Strings

A string is a sequence of alphabets or other characters surrounded by quotation marks, double quotation marks, or triple quotation marks.

Various operations could be done on strings.

In this section, we are going to dig into some of the useful operations.

Example:

```
string_1 = 'civil engineering'
string_2 = "civil engineering"
string_3 = """ if you're going to make Progress in coding, get your hands dirty
Rewrite the codes from scratch"""
```

Chapter 1

NB: If multiple lines constitute the string, it should be surrounded with triple quotation marks.

String length: `len()` function reveals the length of the string.

In
```
len(string_1)
```

Out
17

Slicing: this returns the chosen character.
NB: the first item in Python indexing is 0, not 1.

In
```
string_1[2:9]
```

Out
vil eng

There are 4 built-in data types in Python.
- Lists
- Sets
- Tuple
- Dictionary

List: If we are going to store multiple items in a single variable, then lists are the best choice.
```
list_1 = ['first', 2, 3, 'car']
```

To define a list, a square bracket is needed; moreover, lists are ordered and changeable which will be explained later.

4

Chapter 1

Set: unlike lists, this data type is unordered, without an index, and unalterable. The values, also are written within curly brackets.

Tuple: it is more like a list with some slight differences including unchangeable values and round brackets instead of square brackets.

Dictionary: in this data type, data is stored in key and value pairs as follows.

```
Dictionary_1 = {"steel": 150, "concrete": 100,
                "wood": 50, "aluminum": 40, "plasetic": 35}
```

Now differences in the aforementioned data types will be shown and useful built-in functions would be represented.

Lists and dictionaries

Various functions could be exploited based on the operation you desire. In this section, some fundamental built-in functions will be represented.

NB: remember if you needed a function that is not brought here, just Google it. Many online sites have documented these functions properly.

Lists:

Sort (): **line3**: This function sorts elements in an ascending order.

In

```
line1: list_material = ['steel', 'concrete', 'wood',
line2:                  'aluminum', 'wood', 'steel', 'cement', 'plastic']
line3: list_costs = [150, 100, 50, 40, 50, 150, 30, 35]
line4: list_material.sort()
line5: print(list_material)
```

Out

['aluminum', 'cement', 'concrete', 'plastic', 'steel', 'steel', 'wood', 'wood']

Append and insert: `append()` method adds new elements after the last item in a list, but `insert()` adds new ones to the position you enter:

In

Chapter 1

Line4: `append()`

```
line1: list_material = ['steel', 'concrete', 'wood',
line2:                  'aluminum', 'wood', 'steel', 'cement', 'plastic']
line3: list_costs = [150, 100, 50, 40, 50, 150, 30, 35]
line4: list_material.append('ceramic')
line5: print(list_material)
```

Out
```
['steel', 'concrete', 'wood', 'aluminum', 'wood', 'steel', 'cement', 'plastic', 'ceramic']
```

In
Line 4: `insert()` "tile" after the third place. The first place belongs to "steel".

```
line1: list_material = ['steel', 'concrete', 'wood',
line2:                  'aluminum', 'wood', 'steel', 'cement', 'plastic']
line3: list_costs = [150, 100, 50, 40, 50, 150, 30, 35]
line4: list_material.insert(2, 'tile')
line5: print(list_material)
```

Out
```
['steel', 'concrete', 'tile', 'wood', 'aluminum', 'wood', 'steel', 'cement', 'plastic']
```

Max(), min(): returns the maximum or minimum value in the list

6

Chapter 1

In
```
list_material = ['steel', 'concrete', 'wood',
                 'aluminum', 'wood', 'steel', 'cement', 'plastic']
list_costs = [150, 100, 50, 40, 50, 150, 30, 35]
print(max(list_material))
print(min(list_material))
print(max(list_costs))
print(min(list_costs))
```

Out
```
wood
aluminum
150
30
```

Clear(), pop() and remove()

`clear()` method deletes all the values in a list and returns an empty list.

Both `pop()` and `remove()` remove the element you no longer need; however, in the former, the index should be selected. The latter removes based on the name of the element.

In
Line 4: `clear()`
```
line1: list_material = ['steel', 'concrete', 'wood',
line2:                  'aluminum', 'wood', 'steel', 'cement', 'plastic']
line3: list_costs = [150, 100, 50, 40, 50, 150, 30, 35]
line4: list_material.clear()
line5: print(list_material)
```

Out
```
[]
```

7

Chapter 1

In

Line 4: `pop()` second item of the material list is eliminated

```
line1: list_material = ['steel', 'concrete', 'wood',
line2:                  'aluminum', 'wood', 'steel', 'cement', 'plastic']
line3: list_costs = [150, 100, 50, 40, 50, 150, 30, 35]
line4: list_material.pop(1)
line5: print(list_material)
```

['steel', 'wood', 'aluminum', 'wood', 'steel', 'cement', 'plastic']

In

Line 4: `remove()` – "cement" from the material list is eliminated

```
line1: list_material = ['steel', 'concrete', 'wood',
line2:                  'aluminum', 'wood', 'steel', 'cement', 'plastic']
line3: list_costs = [150, 100, 50, 40, 50, 150, 30, 35]
line4: list_material.remove('cement')
line5: print(list_material)
```

Out
['steel', 'concrete', 'wood', 'aluminum', 'wood', 'steel', 'plastic']

Len(): returns the length of the list

In

```
list_material = ['steel', 'concrete', 'wood',
                 'aluminum', 'wood', 'steel', 'cement', 'plastic']
list_costs = [150, 100, 50, 40, 50, 150, 30, 35]
print(len(list_material))
```

8

Out
8

Count(): this function counts the number of occurrences in a specified element.
In
```
list_material = ['steel', 'concrete', 'wood',
                 'aluminum', 'wood', 'steel', 'cement', 'plastic']
list_costs = [150, 100, 50, 40, 50, 150, 30, 35]
list_material.count('wood')
```

Out
2

The list's features are not limited to the mentioned functions. You can easily iterate through a list with for loops. After defining loops in the upcoming sections, we will get back to the application of loops in lists.

Dictionaries
Get(): this method gets the specified key name and returns the value

In
Line3: prints the whole dictionary
Line4: get () prints the value of the 'wood' key
```
line1: material_cost_dict = {"steel": 150, "concrete": 100,
line2:                        "wood": 50, "aluminum": 40, "plasetic": 35}
line3: print(material_cost_dict)
line4: print(material_cost_dict.get('wood'))
```

Chapter 1

Out
```
{'steel': 150, 'concrete': 100, 'wood': 50, 'aluminum': 40, 'plasetic': 35}

50
```

Keys() and values() :
By applying the `keys()` method, all the keys in our dictionary are shown as a list. Similarly, for `values()`, all the values are displayed.

In
Line4: prints all the keys
Line5: prints all the value

```
line1: material_cost_dict = {"steel": 150, "concrete": 100,
line2:                       "wood": 50, "aluminum": 40, "plasetic": 35}
line3: print(material_cost_dict)
line4: print(material_cost_dict.keys())
line5: print(material_cost_dict.values())
```

Out
```
{'steel': 150, 'concrete': 100, 'wood': 50, 'aluminum': 40, 'plasetic': 35}

dict_keys(['steel', 'concrete', 'wood', 'aluminum', 'plasetic'])

dict_values([150, 100, 50, 40, 35])
```

Pop() and popitem():
`Popitem()` removes the last key and value pair while `pop()` deletes the value of the specified key

10

Chapter 1

In
```python
material_cost_dict = {"steel": 150, "concrete": 100,
                      "wood": 50, "aluminum": 40, "plasetic": 35}
print(material_cost_dict.popitem())
print(material_cost_dict)
```

Out
```
('plasetic', 35)

{'steel': 150, 'concrete': 100, 'wood': 50, 'aluminum': 40}
```

In
```python
material_cost_dict = {"steel": 150, "concrete": 100,
                      "wood": 50, "aluminum": 40, "plasetic": 35}
print(material_cost_dict.pop("steel"))
print(material_cost_dict)
```

Out
```
150

{'concrete': 100, 'wood': 50, 'aluminum': 40, 'plasetic': 35}
```

Update() :

This method inserts a new pair of keys and values into the dictionary. Also, it can be used when a dictionary is going to update another dictionary. Following examples clarify the application of the `update()` method.

11

Chapter 1

In
```
material_cost_dict = {"steel": 150, "concrete": 100,
                      "wood": 50, "aluminum": 40, "plasetic": 35}
print(material_cost_dict.update({"steel": 250}))
print(material_cost_dict)
```

Out
None

{'steel': 250, 'concrete': 100, 'wood': 50, 'aluminum': 40, 'plasetic': 35}

In
```
material_cost_dict_1 = {"steel": 150, "concrete": 100,
                        "wood": 50, "aluminum": 40, "plasetic": 35}
material_cost_dict_2 = {"steel": 250, "concrete": 100,
                        "wood": 50, "aluminum": 40, "plasetic": 35}
(material_cost_dict_1.update(material_cost_dict_2))
print(material_cost_dict_1)
print(material_cost_dict_2)
```

Out

{'steel': 250, 'concrete': 100, 'wood': 50, 'aluminum': 40, 'plasetic': 35}

{'steel': 250, 'concrete': 100, 'wood': 50, 'aluminum': 40, 'plasetic': 35}

If and condition
Well, now an extremely important order in Python is introduced, Decision-making has always been a big part of our brain activity.

Chapter 1

Whether you go to school by bus or bike, whether you drink soda or water, etc. all are everyday routine tasks of our life. This happens exactly when you code.

Based on the logic you pursue; the code is executed as if you are putting a piece of brain in your program.

Now let's get to know the logic, using *if* and related syntaxes.

In

Line1: assigns the x variable to 2
Line2: the first and main condition
Line3: alternative condition
Line 4: the last but optional condition which explicitly takes action when the first and alternative ones are not satisfied.

```
line1: x = 2
line2: if x > 0:
line3:     print('your number is greater than zero')
line4: elif x < 0:
line5:     print('your number is less than zero')
line6: else:
line7:     print('your number is zero')
```

Out
your number is greater than zero

Of course, we all are well aware of the function of *(+), (-), (*), (**), ( ), >, and, or* and *Not* in our real life.

Indeed, these symbols could be traced across hundreds of years of history. Without further ado, a brief of the function of *And, Or,* and *Not* is represented.

And: the statement is true if both of the operands are correct.
Or: if one of the operands is true, the statement is considered true.
Not: this inverts the true statement to a false one.

Chapter 1

In

```
line1: number = int(input('write your number:'))
line2: if number%2==0 and number%3==0:
line3:     print('number is divisible by 6')
line4: elif number%2==0 or number%3==0:
line5:     print('number may be divisible by 6')
line6: elif number==0:
line7:     print('number is zero')
line8: else:
line9:     print("number isn't devisable by 6")
```

Line1: input the number. `Int()` is employed to change the input from string to integer.

Line2: application of *And*. Both of the conditions must be true simultaneously to make the whole argument true.

Line4: application of *Or*. If one of the conditions is true, the whole argument is true.

Out

Test1)

write your number:18

number is divisible by 6

test2)

write your number:15

number may be divisible by 6

test3)

write your number:13

number isn't devisable by 6

Loops and functions

Loop: two major kinds of loops could be selected based on the operation we are going through. A: for loops. B: while loops.

Chapter 1

A) *For loops:* sometimes we need to iterate through elements in lists, sets, tuples, or dictionaries. To do so, as the following example demonstrates *"for loops"* become convenient.

In
```
list_material = ['steel', 'concrete', 'wood',
                 'aluminum', 'wood']
for i in list_material:
    print(i)
```

Out
steel

concrete

wood

aluminum

wood

A-1) *range:* when a programmer wants to repeat the iteration for certain times, `range()` is what they need. Furthermore, generating a desired sequence of values is achievable while using `range(start, end, step-size)` syntax.
NB: Python's indexing system starts from 0.
The following examples could shed light on the concept of loops.

In
```
lst = []
for i in range(0, 10, 2):
    lst.append(i)
print(lst)
```

Chapter 1

Out

[0, 2, 4, 6, 8]

B) *While loops:* In this category of loops, an order is executed until a specific criteria or condition is met.
NB: In a *"while loop"*, iteration may occur for infinite times so, remember to check your condition before embarking on the execution procedure.

In

```
x = 5
lst = []
while x <= 10:
    x = x+1
    lst.append(x)
print(lst)
```

Out

[6, 7, 8, 9, 10, 11]

Function

Consider a situation in which you have a body of codes and some recurrent calculations should be carried out. Functions help you to write your calculation only once and wherever you need the calculation again, the function could be called. For this purpose, the arguments should be passed on to the function and results will emerge.

To pour into details, the next examples will clarify.

In

In this example, a function to find a quadratic equation's roots is prepared.
Line1: when working with mathematical operations including sqrt, sin, and cos the math library must be imported in the first place.
Line3: def arguments are the coefficient of the equation that will be provided by the user.
Line4: here, $\Delta = b^2 - 4ac$ is calculated.
Line5 to 10: evaluate the status of Δ and takes the proper action with:

16

Chapter 1

1. No answer
2. One root
3. Two roots with $x = \dfrac{-b \pm \sqrt{b^2 - 4ac}}{2a}$

In

```
line1:  import math
line2:
line3:  def second_degree_solver(a, b, c):
line4:      delta = (b**2-4*a*c)
line5:      if delta < 0:
line6:          return 'this equation has no real answers'
line7:      elif delta == 0:
line8:          return -b/(2*a)
line9:      else:
line10:         return ((-b+math.sqrt(delta))/(2*a)), ((-b-math.sqrt(delta))/(2*a))
line11:
line12: print(second_degree_solver(1, -4, 3))
```

Out

(3.0, 1.0)

lambda

lambda functions: there is another way of developing a function in Python called *"anonymous functions"*. A.K.A lambda.

There are some merits and drawbacks for lambda which based on the situation of using lambda, makes it beneficial or a burden!

Merits: it's a single-line statement appropriate for short operations.

Demerits: may reduce the readability of the code we cannot use comments on what the defined lambda is doing.

NB: defining a function with def could do whatever lambda does; however, if you want your code to seem professional and chic, lambda would do so.

In

This example is exactly like the previous one with one exception which is being written with lambda.

NB: the "\" sign is used to tell Python that this line is long and the line continues in the next line.

Chapter 1

```
import math

def solver(a, b, c): return (((-b+math.sqrt((b**2-4*a*c)))/(2*a)),
                             ((-b-math.sqrt((b**2-4*a*c)))/(2*a))) if \
                            ((b**2-4*a*c) >= 0) else "no real answer"

print(solver(-1, -3, -20))
```

Out
no real answer

Class

Python is an Object Oriented Programming[1] language. Up until now, whatever example we had, was written in Procedural Programming Order meaning blocks of codes are prepared to carry out a certain of orders.

For example, Python takes a variable from user and does some function on it then you have got the output.

Nevertheless, the whole function must have been written to make your code run. In OOP, the emphasis is on objects and their relation with one another helping you represent real-world things. In fact, by Class, a general behavior that a category can have is produced and this makes you able to use a block of calculation wherever you need even in another program.

This could be much more suitable to avoid the perplexity of the code. Moreover, by using Class you can train your program logically and efficiently.

In terms of detailed syntaxes, full online documentation of the Class could be reached at www.python.org. Here, we do not get involved in details meanwhile useful features plus general syntaxes are discussed. We strongly recommend mastering the details for enthusiasts.

Like real-world events, we have objects called instantiation and functions named methods.

Now with a few examples, we try to clear up this mess a bit!

---

[1] OOP

Chapter 1

In
```python
import math

class simple_statistics:
    def __init__(self, a, b, c):
        self.a = a
        self.b = b
        self.c = c

    def average(self):
        value_aveg = (self.a+self.b+self.c)/3
        return value_aveg

    def square_root(self):
        sq_rt = math.sqrt((self.a)**2+(self.b)**2+(self.c)**2)
        return sq_rt

test_1 = simple_statistics(1, 2, 3)
print(test_1.average())
print(round(simple_statistics(5, 9, 10).square_root(),3))
```

Out
2.0

14.353

Exception/ error handling
Syntax error
An inevitable part of programming especially for beginners is facing syntax error. In this case, the code cannot be executed as if you have been mistaken in using or not using something. Therefore, there are no results unless you find the flaw in your program and correct it.

Chapter 1

In
```
value_1=1256
value_2=value_1*/2
print(value_2)
```

Out
  value_2=value_1*/2

         ^

SyntaxError: invalid syntax

Exception

When codes are written carefully without syntax errors, some other errors may raise. These errors are called *"Exception"* and may disrupt the flow of codes. A developer should learn to handle them if they want an errorless code.

Exception	description
Index Error	When the wrong index of a list is retrieved
Assertion Error	It occurs when the assert statement fails
Attribute Error	It occurs when an attribute assignment fails
Import Error	It occurs when an imported module is not found
Key Error	It occurs when the key of the dictionary is not found
Name Error	It occurs when the variable is not defined
Memory Error	It occurs when a program runs out of memory
Type Error	It occurs when a function and operation are applied in an incorrect type
Zero division Error	It occurs when the denominator is zero

Chapter 1

Handling exception

The main structure is as below:
Try:
>Code block

Exception:
>Code block

Else:
>Code block

Finally:
>Code block

Often *try* and *exception* are enough for error handling.

In
```python
def divide(x, y):
    try:
        result = x // y
        print("Your answer is :", result)
    except ZeroDivisionError:
        print('You are dividing by zero')

divide(3, 0)
```

Out
You are dividing by zero

Opening/closing files

One of the elementary particles of coding is handling files. In numerous circumstances, a programmer should open or close files. As an example: a researcher working with historical data of stock markets always has to struggle with tons of data in CSV, json, or text formats. If she decides to automate a part of her research, then opening and manipulating data sets would be inevitable.

Moreover, if the very researcher tends to store the outputs of her calculation, she should open an external file and write or append whatever her work is.

To do so, in this part, this important section of programming is addressed.

Two methods are feasible when it comes to file handling.

Simple open method which necessitates the close command.

Chapter 1

With the open method in which you no longer need use close commands.
In this book, we go with the second approach simply because often files remain open and we forget to use close command!

Operation	Syntax	Description
Read Only	r	Open text file for reading only.
Read and Write	r+	Open the file for reading and writing.
Write Only	w	Open the file for writing.
Write and Read	w+	Open the file for reading and writing. Unlike "r+" it doesn't raise an I/O error if the file doesn't exist.
Append Only	a	Open the file for writing and create es new file if it doesn't exist. All additions are made at the end of the file and no existing data can be modified.
Append and Read	a+	Open the file for reading and writing and create s new file if it doesn't exist. All additions are made at the end of the file and no existing data can be modified.

In

```
with open('file.txt', 'r') as file_1:
    print(file_1.read())
```

Chapter 1

Out

toranj 80

tileh 75

miasha 70

james 25

john 30

scarlet 50

deb 84

In

```python
with open('file.txt', 'a') as file_1:
    print(file_1.write('brojes 20'))
```

Out

toranj 80

tileh 75

misha 70

james 25

john 30

scarlet 50

deb 84

brojes 20

Chapter 1

Mixed Examples

Example 1: Write a Python program to get a string made of the first 2 and last 2 characters of a given string. If the string length is less than 2, return the "empty" phrase.

```python
word = input('write your word:')
if len(word) <= 2:
    print('empty')
else:
    word_modified = word[0]+word[1]+word[-2]+word[-1]
    print(word_modified)
```

Example 2: write a program to change the alphabet of a string to uppercase if it is lowercase and vice versa.

```python
name = input('name')
lst = []
lst1 = []
for i in name:
    if i.isupper() == True:
        lst.append(i.lower())
    elif i.islower() == True:
        lst.append(i.upper())
print(''.join(str(x) for x in lst))
```

Example 3: Write a Python program that takes a string and replaces all the characters with their respective numbers.

```python
word = input('write your word:')
numbers_list = []
for i in word:
    numbers_list.append(ord(i))

print(numbers_lists)
```

24

Chapter 1

Example 4: Write a Python function that takes a list of words and returns the longest word and the length of the longest one.

```python
def longest_word(words_lists):
    word_len = []
    for i in words_lists:
        word_len.append((len(i), i))
    word_len.sort()
    return word_len[-1]

print(longest_word(["cement", "grout", "bar"]))
```

Mini project: Random walk

Random walk in probability is a process by which a wanderer embarks upon a random decision-making operation. Considering a confused ant after losing track of others would clarify the theory.

Given the initial direction selected by the ant and random decisions afterward, a path is formed after hundreds of steps. Firstly, we generate these walks and secondly, we draw the path using the matplotlib package which will be addressed properly in upcoming chapters.

Random walks have application in many fields, ranging from biology to stock market-trends.

25

Chapter 1

Procedural approach:

```python
import random
import matplotlib.pyplot as plt
lst = [-4, -3, -2, -1, 0, 1, 2, 3, 4]
x = 0
y = 0
lst1 = []
lst2 = []
for i in range(0, 500):
    x = x+random.choice(lst)
    y = y+random.choice(lst)

    lst1.append(x)
    lst2.append(y)

plt.scatter(lst1, lst2)
plt.show()
```

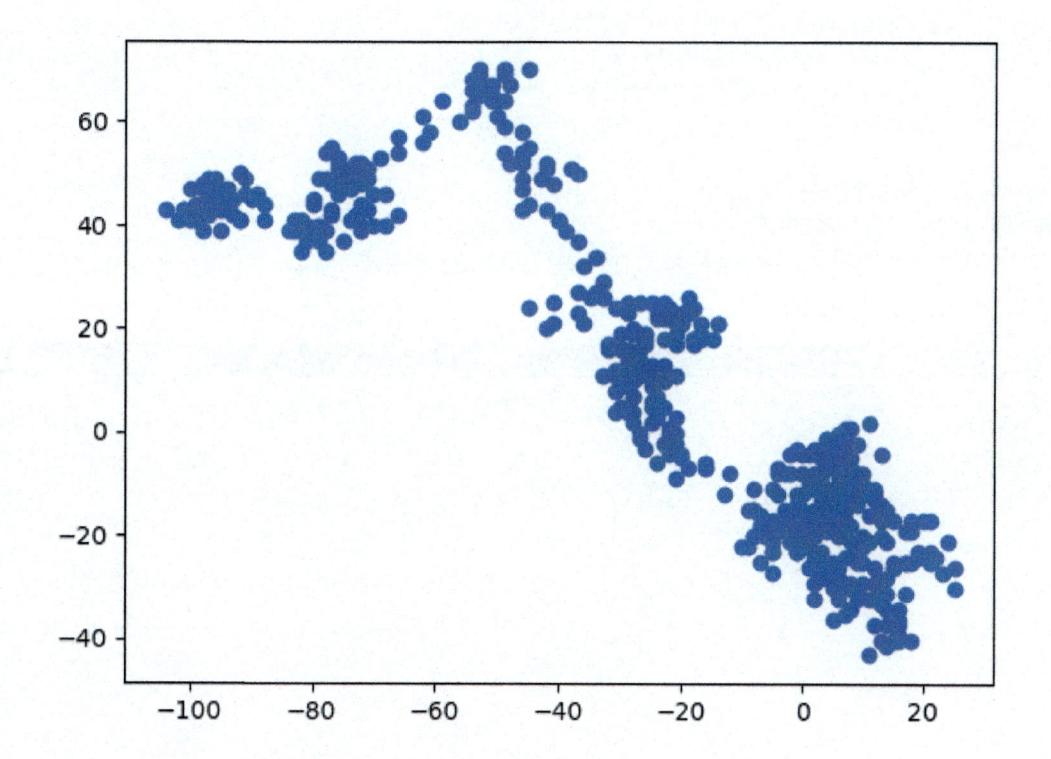

Chapter 1

Object-oriented approach:

```python
class Randomwalk:
    def __init__(self, walksnumber=500):
        self.walksnumber = walksnumber
        self.x_values = [0]
        self.y_values = [0]

    def mainfunction(self):

        while len(self.x_values) < self.walksnumber:

            x_dir = choice([1, -1])
            y_dir = choice([1, -1])
            x_distance = choice([0, 1, 2, 3, 4])
            y_distance = choice([0, 1, 2, 3, 4])
            x_step = x_dir*x_distance
            y_step = y_dir*y_distance
            if x_step == 0 and y_step == 0:
                continue
            x = self.x_values[-1]+x_step
            y = self.y_values[-1]+y_step
            self.x_values.append(x)
            self.y_values.append(y)


sample_1 = Randomwalk()
sample_1.mainfunction()
plt.scatter(sample_1.x_values, sample_1.y_values)
plt.show()
```

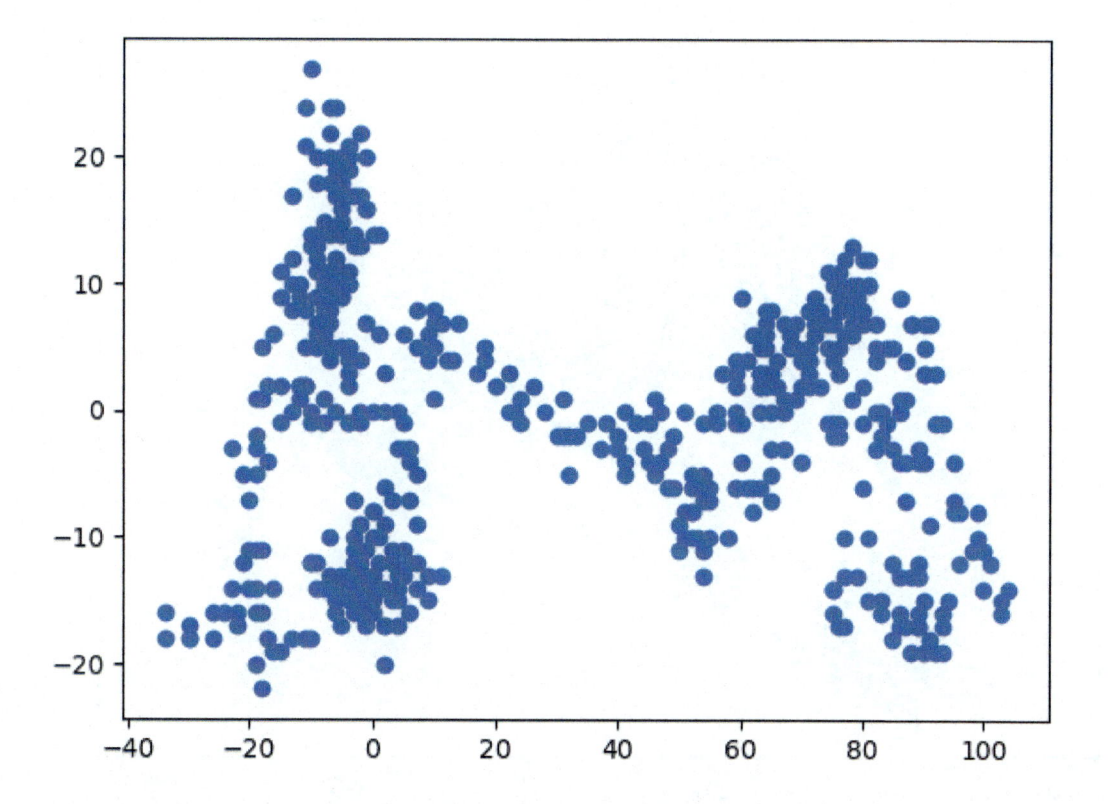

Chapter 1

Easier OOP with an arbitrary number of walks:

```python
class Randomwalk:
    def __init__(self, walksnumber):
        self.walksnumber = walksnumber
        self.x_values = [0]
        self.y_values = [0]
        self.lst = [-4, -3, -2, -1, 0, 1, 2, 3, 4]

    def mainfunction(self):

        for i in range(1, self.walksnumber+1):

            x = self.x_values[-1]+random.choice(self.lst)
            y = self.y_values[-1]+random.choice(self.lst)
            self.x_values.append(x)
            self.y_values.append(y)

sample_1 = Randomwalk(1000)
sample_1.mainfunction()
plt.scatter(sample_1.x_values, sample_1.y_values)
plt.show()
```

Chapter 1

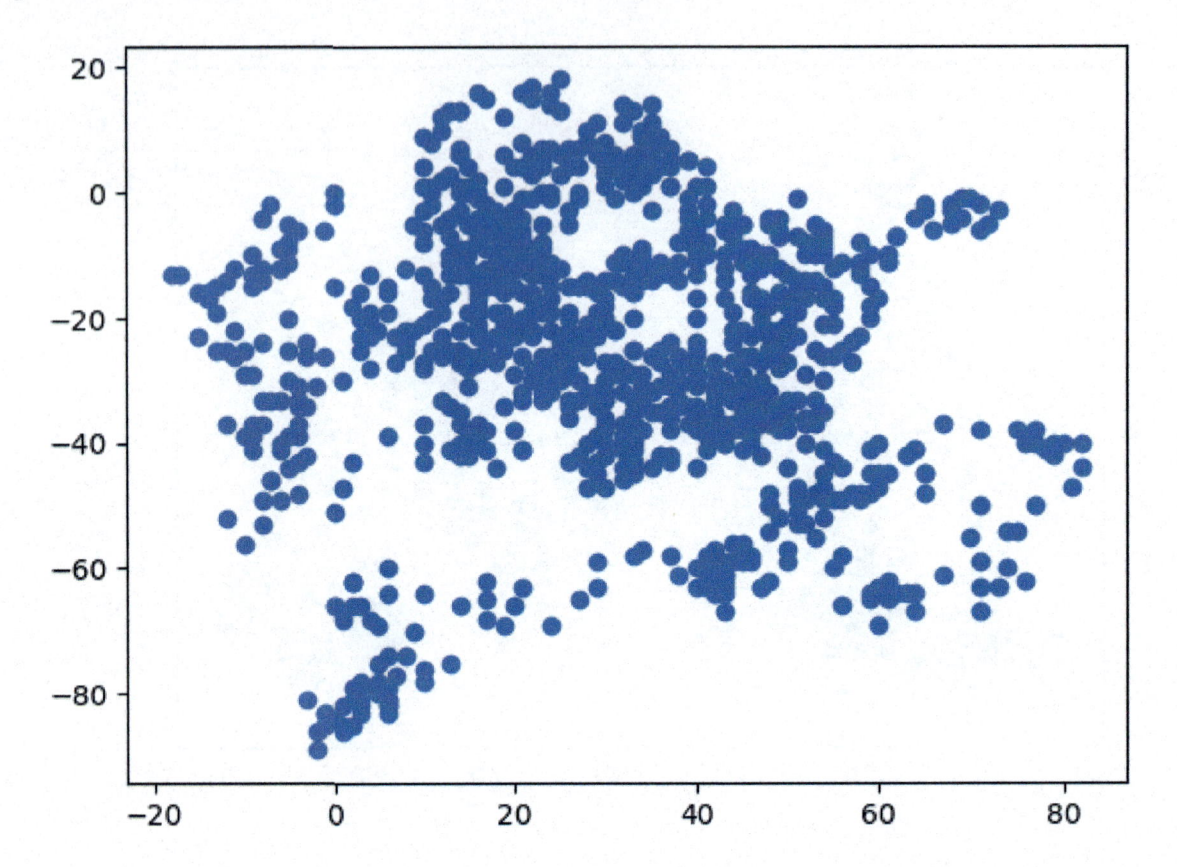

Chapter 2

Chapter 2

In the second part of this book, expedient libraries are to be explained. Libraries could be defined as a group or collection of models that provide developers with golden opportunities to save time, money, and effort.

The libraries make coding easier not because some smart people have collected models together, but rather due to the convenience of using them in all your works. What's more, THEY ARE FREE! So let's get familiar with some astonishingly useful libraries.

Numpy

You may have thought of forming matrixes or operating mathematical functions with numbers and values in Python. Surely you can take advantage of lists or other data types. But here's the thing, Numpy arrays are much faster and easy to work with when it comes to scientific computations.

This open-source library has some flaws though, for example, lists seem a proper choice where different data types should be stored. Having said that, in this context which is *"civil engineering calculation"*, Numpy would be a better choice. Related syntaxes and useful features of Numpy will be discussed but before that, how to install Numpy? All installation procedures including Python itself, pip, IDEs, and libraries are covered in appendixes.

Although we're going to debate over the extremely useful functions of Numpy, they are not scrutinized since they will demand copious notes and documents, which unnecessarily makes this book ticker. So if you need a certain function that is not covered in this book, just google it. Full online documentation of Numpy is available at Numpy.org.

Creating arrays

Numpy provides a vast variety of methods to build an array. One-dimensional array and two-dimensional array are created as example 1 illustrates.

In:
Line1: creates a 1*3 array
Line2: creates a 2*3 array

Chapter 2

```
line1: print(np.array([1, 2, 3]))
line2: print(np.array([(1, 2, 3), (3, 2, 1)]))
```

Out:
array([1, 2, 3])

array([[1, 2, 3],
       [3, 2, 1]])

Sometimes we need arrays of zeros or ones. We can create them like example 1, but it would be either time-consuming or confusing.

For this purpose, Numpy comes up with a solution, shown in example 2. Based on the formation of zeros or ones or any other numbers, one could use the example 2 methods and avoid writing ones repeatedly!

In:
Line1: creates 5*4 array of zeros
Line2: creates 2*5 array of ones

```
line1: print(np.zeros((5, 4)))
line2: print(np.ones((2, 5)))
```

Out:
array([[0., 0., 0., 0.],
       [0., 0., 0., 0.],
       [0., 0., 0., 0.],
       [0., 0., 0., 0.],
       [0., 0., 0., 0.]])

array([[1., 1., 1., 1., 1.],
       [1., 1., 1., 1., 1.]])

Numpy can also constitute an array from a start point to an endpoint with the desired number of values. On the other hand, Numpy can organize an array with constant steps from a start point to an endpoint.

In:
Line1: linearly divides 0 to 11 to 10 values
Line2: linearly divides 0 to 11 to 10 values and rounds the values with 3 decimals
Line3: forms an array of numbers starting with 0 by 45.2 increment step to 300
Line4: creates 3*5 array with constant values of 10

```
line1: print(np.linspace(0, 11, 10))
line2: print(np.around(np.linspace(0, 11, 10), 3))
line3: print(np.arange(15, 300, 45.2))
line4: print(np.full((3, 5), 10))
```

Out:
line1: [0.   1.22222222 2.44444444 3.66666667 4.88888889 6.11111111

line1:   7.33333333 8.55555556 9.77777778 11.   ]

line2: [0.   1.222 2.444 3.667 4.889 6.111 7.333 8.556 9.778 11.   ]

line3: [15.   60.2 105.4 150.6 195.8 241. 286.2]

line4: [[10 10 10 10 10]

line4: [10 10 10 10 10]

line4: [10 10 10 10 10]]

Many calculations demand arrays of randomly selected values. Whether the values are integer or float, the proper method could be chosen.
In:

Chapter 2

Line1: generate a 3*5 array of random floats between 0 to 100
Line1: generate a 5*58 array of random integers between 0 to 23

```
line1: print(np.around((np.random.rand(3, 5)*100), 3))
line2: print(np.random.randint(23, size=(5, 8)))
```

Out:
line1: [[85.53 61.335 36.053 54.605 7.342]

line1: [44.372 70.005 69.822 1.011 19.658]

line1: [96.595 14.92 53.965 57.432 9.946]]

line2: [[4 16 4 13 5 8 4 16]

line2: [18 14 6 21 17 4 6 8]

line2: [11 22 4 1 7 13 5 13]

line2: [15 6 9 1 16 11 14 9]

line2: [22 10 16 4 8 3 21 10]]

Indexing
You may want access to one of the values inside an array for your calculations. Just like lists, Numpy could return values easily.
In:
Line1-9: creates an array (matrix)
Line11: prints the third row
Line13: prints the value in the second row and the fourth column
Line15: prints the value in the second row and the fourth column
Line17: prints the value in the first row to the third only for the third column
Line19: prints the values in the first row and the second rows
Line21: prints the values in the third column
Line23: check if the values are bigger than five or not
Line25: prints all values below five

33

Chapter 2

```
line1 : ar = np.array([[0,  4,  1,  2, 12,  3, 11, 19],
line2 :
line3 :               [16, 15, 17,  6, 11, 20,  1,  8],
line4 :
line5 :               [2, 21,  3, 20,  8, 17, 19, 12],
line6 :
line7 :               [4,  4, 21, 14, 11,  3,  8, 19],
line8 :
line9 :               [9,  0, 20,  4,  2,  7,  5, 10]])
line10:
line11: print(ar[2])
line12:
line13: print(ar[1, 3])
line14:
line15: print(ar[0:3])
line16:
line17: print(ar[0:3, 2])
line18:
line19: print(ar[:2])
line20:
line21: print(ar[:, 2])
line22:
line23: print(ar < 5)
line24:
line25: print(ar[ar < 5])
```

Out:

34

Chapter 2

line11 : [2 21 3 20 8 17 19 12]

line13 : 6

line15 : [[0 4 1 2 12 3 11 19]

line15 : [16 15 17 6 11 20 1 8]

line15 : [2 21 3 20 8 17 19 12]]

line17 : [1 17 3]

line19: [[0 4 1 2 12 3 11 19]

line19: [16 15 17 6 11 20 1 8]]

line21: [1 17 3 21 20]

line23: [[True True True True False True False False]

line23: [False False False False False False True False]

line23: [True False True False False False False False]

line23: [True True False False False True False False]

line23: [False True False True True False False False]]

line25: [0 4 1 2 3 1 2 3 4 4 3 0 4 2]

If you want to change a value within an array, you could assign the new value to the intended index.

In:
```
a_matrix = np.array([2, 3, 54, 6, 7, 8])
a_matrix[2] = 32
print(a_matrix)
```

Out:
[2 3 32 6 7 8]

Chapter 2

In:

```
a_matrix = np.array([[2, 3, 54],
                     [6, 7, 8]])
a_matrix[1, 2] = 32
print(a_matrix)
```

Out:

[[2 3 54]

 [6 7 32]]

Properties
Often we should check out the size, shape, or even data type of the arrays. These syntaxes are demonstrated in the following example.

In:
Line3: prints the shape of the matrix
Line4: prints the total number of values in the matrix
Line5: prints type of values in the matrix

```
line1: a_matrix = np.array([[2, 3, 54],
line2:                      [6, 7.5, 8]])
line3: print(a_matrix.shape)
line4: print(a_matrix.size)
line5: print(a_matrix.dtype)
```

Out:

36

Chapter 2

Line3: (2, 3)

Line4: 6

Line5: float64

Combining or splitting

For many reasons, we may want to add an array to another existing array. Given where we want this new array to be added, the axis could be chosen.

In:
```python
array_1 = np.array([[2, 3, 54],
                    [6, 7.5, 8]])
array_2 = np.array([[1, 2, 65],
                    [7.5, 1.5, 8]])

print(np.concatenate((array_1, array_2), axis=0))
print(np.concatenate((array_1, array_2), axis=1))
```

Out:

[[2. 3. 54.]

 [6. 7.5 8.]

 [1. 2. 65.]

 [7.5 1.5 8.]]

[[2. 3. 54. 1. 2. 65.]

 [6. 7.5 8. 7.5 1.5 8.]]

If an array should be split into sub-arrays, there are built-in functions.

In:

37

```python
a_matrix = np.array([[2, 3, 54],
                     [6, 7.5, 8]])
print(np.split(a_matrix, 2))
print(np.hsplit(a_matrix, 3))
```

Out:
[array([[2., 3., 54.]]), array([[6. , 7.5, 8.]])]

[array([[2.],

   [6.]]), array([[3.],

   [7.5]]), array([[54.],

   [8.]])]

Basic math

We talked about the convenience of Numpy in numerical calculations, some fundamental operations are illustrated in example 11.

https://numpy.org/doc/stable/reference/routines.math.html

In:
Line1-5: defining the arrays and lists
Line6-7: sum of all elements in `arr_1` and specified list
Line8-9: maximum and minimum of the elements in `arr_1`
Line10: mean of the `arr_1` elements
Line11-13: sinus, cosinus, and tangent of the elements in `angles_list`
Line14: first changes the radian to a degree and then calculate the sinus
Line15: the exponential value of the array
Line16: logarithm of the values of an array
Line17: an absolute value of the numbers in the array

Chapter 2

```
line1 : arr_1 = np.array([1, 2, 3, 4])
line2 : arr_2 = np.array([5, 6, 7, 8])
line3 : arr_3 = np.array([-5, -6, -7, -8])
line4 : lst_1 = [1, 2.5, 3.5, 4]
line5 : angles_list = [30, 45, 60, 63]
line6 : print(np.sum(arr_1))
line7 : print(np.sum(([1, 2, 3])))
line8 : print(np.max(arr_1))
line9 : print(np.min(arr_1))
line10: print(np.mean(arr_1))
line11: print(np.sin(angles_list))
line12: print(np.cos(angles_list))
line13: print(np.tan(angles_list))
line14: print(np.sin(np.rad2deg(angles_list)))
line15: print(np.exp(arr_1))
line16: print(np.log10(arr_1))
line17: print(np.absolute(arr_3))
```

Out:

Chapter 2

10

6

4

1

2.5

[-0.98803162 0.85090352 -0.30481062 0.1673557]

[0.15425145 0.52532199 -0.95241298 0.98589658]

[-6.4053312   1.61977519 0.32004039 0.16974975]

[-0.4097718   0.80607549 0.74757789 0.05582062]

[2.71828183 7.3890561 20.08553692 54.59815003]

[0.   0.30103   0.47712125 0.60205999]

[5 6 7 8]

Math (intermediate)
In this section, more complicated mathematical methods are investigated. Most of the mathematical functions are known by the audience of this book, but some quick additional hints will be given, if necessary.

Besides, all of them are placed in the linear algebra category.

Polyfit-root-eighenvalue-percentile-std-var-img-eye-fromfunction

Equation's roots:
In this function, first of all, the coefficients of the equation are determined and placed in a list. Then with upcoming roots, the roots will be calculated.

In:

Here is the equation:

$x^3 - 6x^2 + 11x - 6$

Chapter 2

```
coeff = [1, -6, 11, -6]
print(np.roots(coeff))
```

Out:
[3. 2. 1.]

Linear algebra
This method computes the exact solution of x. if a matrix is square and of full rank. Simultaneously, all rows and columns must be linearly independent.
NB: square matrix is a matrix with an equivalent number of rows and columns.
NB: full rank matrix means the matrix has the high possible rank for a same-size matrix.

In:
The equations to solve are:
$x_0 + 2x_1 = 1$
$3x_0 + 5x_1 = 2$

Therefore, the matrixes are:
$$a = \begin{pmatrix} 1 & 2 \\ 3 & 5 \end{pmatrix}$$

$$b = \begin{pmatrix} 1 \\ 2 \end{pmatrix}$$

```
a = np.array([[1, 2], [3, 5]])
b = np.array([1, 2])
x = np.linalg.solve(a, b)
```

This example is directly from Numpy official documentation.

Out:
[-1. 1.]

Chapter 2

Polyfit

It is used to calculate the Least squares polynomial fit of given data.

In:

`Y_test` here is used to test if the value of the `coeff_calculation` is correct.

```python
x = np.linspace(0, 20, 5)
y_test = 2*x**3+3*x**2+1
coeff_calculation = np.polyfit(x, y_test, 3)
print(coeff_calculation)
```

Out:

[2.00000000e+00 3.00000000e+00 -2.65680408e-12 1.00000000e+00]

Eigenvalue

You may ask why on earth we should learn eigenvalues. Well, the short answer is wherever matrixes emerge; eigenvalues inexorably pop up.

In a seismic design where we encounter mass, damping, deformation, and stiffness matrixes, through the well. Known formula of $m\ddot{u}+c\dot{u}+ku=P(t)$ the main frequency of the structure is calculated by eigenvalues of the matrix.

In addition, in strength of materials eigenvalues of the stress tensor are main stress A.K.A, S11, S22, and S33. Fortunately, Numpy facilitates this calculation.

In:

```python
m = np.matrix("3 -2;1 0")
print('the main matrix is:\n', m)
w, v = np.linalg.eig(m)
print('the Eigenvalue value is:\n', w)
print('the vector is:\n', v)
```

Out:

Chapter 2

the main matrix is:

[[3 -2]

[1 0]]

the Eigenvalue value is:

[2. 1.]

the vector is:

[[0.89442719 0.70710678]

[0.4472136 0.70710678]]

Import and export

Some data may be derived from other sources such as *Abaqus* or *Etabs*, which are extremely practical software in structural, engineering and you want to export this data to Python since you have figured out that working with data is a piece of cake in Python.

For this purpose, given what the format of your data is, a few methods are devised for both exporting and importing.

In:
```python
arr_1 = np.random.randint(50, size=25)
print(arr_1)
np.savetxt('test.txt', arr_1, delimiter=' ')
```

Out:
This will create a text file with values of arr_1.

In:
```python
np.loadtxt('test.txt')
```

Out:
This will import values from a text file called test.txt.

`Savetxt` and `loadtxt` can have more arguments including the delimiter, path, etc., which are available in the documentation at numpy.org

Mini project

In this mini project linear regression with the least square method will be discussed and related code will be developed.

$$y = a + bx + \varepsilon$$

Where should be minimized. After some calculations, the results are:

$$b = \frac{n\sum xy - (\sum x)(\sum y)}{n\sum x^2 - (\sum x)^2}$$

$$a = \frac{\sum y - b(\sum x)}{n}$$

```python
import numpy as np
x = np.array([1, 2, 3])
y = 2*x+1
n = len(x)
b = (n*np.sum(x*y)-np.sum(x)*np.sum(y))/(n*np.sum(x**2)-(np.sum(x))**2)
a = (np.sum(y)-b*np.sum(x))/n
print('a is:\n', a)
print('b is:\n', b)
```

a is:

1.0

b is:

2.0

Chapter 3

Pandas

According to pandas.org. *"pandas"* is a fast, powerful, flexible and easy to use open source data analysis and manipulation tool, which is built based on Python programming language".

Actually, pandas is where you can store and change data. You can also do statistics with columns and rows and eventually, you may plot the data. A serious question is posed here: *"Why should we use pandas over Excel?"*

Well, Excel would be a proper choice if the project is not dealing with a huge amount of data, since it may get too long to process the data. On the contrary, numerous tasks could be automated via pandas which makes you avoid tedious tasks from Excel.

Creating DataFrames

It is like a spreadsheet constituting of columns and rows. There are three major methods to form the DataFrame.

From a dictionary:

In this method, a dictionary is built outside or inside the DataFrame command and it specifics the values for columns.

`Syntax:`
`DataFrame.from_dict(data, orient='columns', dtype=None, columns=None)`

In

```python
import pandas as pd
data = {'materials': ['steel', 'concrete', 'glass'], 'elastic modulus(GPa)': [
    210, 15, 50]}
df = pd.DataFrame.from_dict(data)
print(df)
```

Out

	materials	elastic modulus(GPa)
0	steel	210
1	concrete	15
2	glass	50

From arrays:
In this method, arrays specify the values of each row, followed by columns names.

In
```
data = {'row_1': ['steel', 210], 'row_2': [
    'concrete', 15], 'row_3': ['glass', 50]}
df = pd.DataFrame.from_dict(data, orient='index')
print(df)
```

Out

	0	1
row_1	steel	210
row_2	concrete	15
row_3	glass	50

Form a list:
This method uses a single or a list of lists to compose a DataFrame.

Chapter 3

In
```
material_lst = ['steel', 'concrete', 'glass']
elastic_modulus_lst = [210,15,50]
df = pd.DataFrame(list(zip(material_lst, elastic_modulus_lst)),
            columns =['Name', 'value'])
print(df)
```

Out

	name	value
0	steel	210
1	concrete	15
2	glass	50

To make it clear, a real-world DataFrame called *"worldwide earthquake"* from Kaggle.com is downloaded and subjected to changes in the following methods.

Loading the database

In
```
import pandas as pd
import numpy as np
eq_df = pd.read_csv('Worldwide_Earthquake_database.csv')
```

Chapter 3

Out
NB: Rows and columns are interchanged for display purposes.

	0	**1**	**2**	**3**	**4**
I_D	1	2	3	5877	8
FLAG_TSUNAMI	No	Yes	No	Yes	No
YEAR	-2150	-2000	-2000	-1610	-1566
MONTH					
DAY					
HOUR					
MINUTE					
SECOND					
FOCAL_DEPTH			18		
EQ_PRIMARY	7.3		7.1		
EQ_MAG_MW					
EQ_MAG_MS			7.1		
EQ_MAG_MB					
EQ_MAG_ML					
EQ_MAG_MFA					
EQ_MAG_UNK	7.3				
INTENSITY		10	10		10
COUNTRY	JORDAN	SYRIA	TURKMENISTAN	GREECE	ISRAEL
STATE					
LOCATION_NAME	JORDAN: BAB-A-DARAA,AL-KARAK	SYRIA: UGARIT	TURKMENISTAN: W	GREECE: THERA ISLAND (SANTORINI)	ISRAEL: ARIHA (JERICHO)
LATITUDE	31.1	35.683	38	36.4	31.5
LONGITUDE	35.5	35.8	58.2	25.4	35.3
REGION_CODE	140	130	40	130	140
DEATHS			1		
DEATHS_DESCRIPTION		3	1		
MISSING					
MISSING_DESCRIPTION					
INJURIES					
INJURIES_DESCRIPTION					
DAMAGE_MILLIONS_DOLLARS					
DAMAGE_DESCRIPTION	3		1		3
HOUSES_DESTROYED					
HOUSES_DESTROYED_DESCRIPTION			1		
HOUSES_DAMAGED					
HOUSES_DAMAGED_DESCRIPTION					

Chapter 3

TOTAL_DEATHS			1		
TOTAL_DEATHS_DESCRIPTION		3	1	3	
TOTAL_MISSING					
TOTAL_MISSING_DESCRIPTION					
TOTAL_INJURIES					
TOTAL_INJURIES_DESCRIPTION					
TOTAL_DAMAGE_MILLIONS_DOLLARS					
TOTAL_DAMAGE_DESCRIPTION			1	3	
TOTAL_HOUSES_DESTROYED					
TOTAL_HOUSES_DESTROYED_DESCRIPTION			1		
TOTAL_HOUSES_DAMAGED					
TOTAL_HOUSES_DAMAGED_DESCRIPTION					

Drop method

The database contains some records columns and rows that we are willing to drop due to the existence of unnecessary data or Nan values. The full syntax for this purpose is.

```
df.drop(labels: IndexLabel=, Axis=, index: IndexLabel=,
columns: IndexLabel=, Level=..., inplace: Literal[True],
errors: IgnoreRaise=...)
```

For example, this is how it is implemented:

Chapter 3

In

```python
eq_df_m = eq_df.drop(labels=['STATE', 'LOCATION_NAME', 'LATITUDE', 'LONGITUDE', 'REGION_CODE',
                              'DEATHS_DESCRIPTION', 'MISSING', 'MISSING_DESCRIPTION', 'INJURIES', 'INJURIES_DESCRIPTION',
                              'DAMAGE_MILLIONS_DOLLARS', 'DAMAGE_DESCRIPTION', 'HOUSES_DESTROYED', 'HOUSES_DESTROYED_DESCRIPTION',
                              'HOUSES_DAMAGED', 'HOUSES_DAMAGED_DESCRIPTION', 'TOTAL_DEATHS_DESCRIPTION',
                              'TOTAL_MISSING', 'TOTAL_MISSING_DESCRIPTION', 'TOTAL_INJURIES', 'TOTAL_INJURIES_DESCRIPTION',
                              'TOTAL_DAMAGE_MILLIONS_DOLLARS', 'TOTAL_DAMAGE_DESCRIPTION', 'TOTAL_HOUSES_DESTROYED',
                              'TOTAL_HOUSES_DESTROYED_DESCRIPTION',
                              'TOTAL_HOUSES_DAMAGED', 'TOTAL_HOUSES_DAMAGED_DESCRIPTION', 'EQ_MAG_MB',
                              'EQ_MAG_ML', 'EQ_MAG_MFA', 'EQ_MAG_UNK', 'SECOND', 'MINUTE','DEATHS'], axis=1,
                     errors='ignore')
rowstoremove = np.arange(0, 2909, 1)
print(rowstoremove)
df = eq_df_m.drop(rowstoremove)
```

Out

First 5 rows of elimination

	FLAG_TSUNAMI	YEAR	MONTH	DAY	HOUR	FOCAL_DEPTH	EQ_PRIMARY	EQ_MAG_MW	EQ_MAG_MS	INTENSITY	COUNTRY	TOTAL_DEATHS
0	No	-2150					7.3				JORDAN	
1	Yes	-2000								10	SYRIA	
2	No	-2000				18	7.1		7.1	10	TURKMENISTAN	1
3	Yes	-1610									GREECE	
4	No	-1566								10	ISRAEL	

Chapter 3

Out

First 5 rows of after eliminating rows

	FLAG_TSUNAMI	YEAR	MONTH	DAY	HOUR	FOCAL_DEPTH	EQ_PRIMARY	EQ_MAG_MW	EQ_MAG_MS	INTENSITY	COUNTRY	TOTAL_DEATHS
2909	Yes	1920	9	20	14	35	7.8	7.8	7.9		NEW CALEDONIA	
2910	No	1920	11	26	8	25	6.2	6.2		11	ALBANIA	200
2911	Yes	1920	12	16	12	25	8.3	8.3	8.6	12	CHINA	200000
2912	No	1920	12	17	18	10	6		6	8	ARGENTINA	400
2913	Yes	1920	12	18	2		5.6		5.6	9	ALBANIA	

Columns to drop

- Columns that are to be dropped are listed before **the** `labels` argument.
    - `Axis=1` is to tell Python that these are columns to be dropped. If the `Axis=0` was selected, then this would have led to nothing as these labels are not found in the rows (indexes).
    - `Errors='ignore'` means hey python if the is a misspelling in the labels names or any of the written names in the labels list, just ignore it and do whatever is ordered to existing values.

Rows to drop

- This dataset also contains some ancient records from 2150 BC that is useless for our purpose, so we shall drop them too. Up until record row number 2909 is before 1920 and do not want them. So that a very similar process to columns should be done with a slight difference which is `Axis=1`. By the way, if you don't write down the `Axis=0` argument it's going to be ok as the default value in the argument is defined zero.

Chapter 3

Dropping Nan values
```
df = df.dropna(subset=['YEAR', 'MONTH', 'DAY'])
```

- This means drop related rows, if there is a Nan(undefined value) value in the subset of:
['YEAR', 'MONTH', 'DAY']

Date and time
In many databases like this, Hour, Minute, and Second are brought in separate columns. Here we wish to join them and make onecolumns as the representative of date.

In
```
line1:df['MONTH'] = df['MONTH'].astype(int)
line2:df['DAY'] = df['DAY'].astype(int)
line3:df['date'] = df['YEAR'].astype(
line4:    str)+str('/')+df['MONTH'].astype(str)+
line5:    str('/')+df['DAY'].astype(str)
line6:
line7:df['date'] = pd.to_datetime(df['date'])
line8:df = df.drop(labels=['YEAR', 'MONTH', 'DAY'], axis=1)
```

Out
First 5 rows of fixed data and time

	FLAG_TSUNAMI	HOUR	FOCAL_DEPTH	EQ_PRIMARY	EQ_MAG_MW	EQ_MAG_MS	INTENSITY	COUNTRY	TOTAL_DEATHS	Date
2909	Yes	14	35	7.8	7.8	7.9		NEW CALEDONIA		1920-09-20 00:00:00
2910	No	8	25	6.2	6.2		11	ALBANIA	200	1920-11-26 00:00:00
2911	Yes	12	25	8.3	8.3	8.6	12	CHINA	200000	1920-12-16 00:00:00
2912	No	18	10	6		6	8	ARGENTINA	400	1920-12-17 00:00:00
2913	Yes	2		5.6		5.6	9	ALBANIA		1920-12-18 00:00:00
2914	No	17					12	ITALY		1921-01-13 00:00:00

Chapter 3

Line1-Line2: To join values in a pandas DataFrame, all values should be sa tring but before that, allnumbersr should change to integers to eliminate decimal points.

Line3-Line5: Then all of the aforementioned values gather together after changing to strings.

Line6: With basic method of `pd.to_datetime()`,values in our new column date are in datetime type.

Line7: Eventually having three columns in a single column (date) leads to dropping Year, Month and Day.

Relocation of columns

If the location of columns needs to change, then we should be able to move columns into our desirable arrangement. In this example, we want 'DATA', 'HOUR', ' EQ_PRIMARY', 'COUNTRY' and 'TOTAL_DEATHS' be placed in the first, second, third, fourth and fifth columns respectively.

In

```python
first_col = df.pop('date')
df.insert(0, 'date', first_col)
second_col = df.pop('HOUR')
df.insert(1, 'HOUR', second_col)
third_col = df.pop('EQ_PRIMARY')
df.insert(2, 'EQ_PRIMARY', third_col)
forth_col = df.pop('COUNTRY')
df.insert(3, 'COUNTRY', forth_col)
fifth_col = df.pop('TOTAL_DEATHS')
df.insert(4, 'TOTAL_DEATHS', fifth_col)
```

Chapter 3

Out
First 5 rows with relocated columns

	Date	HOUR	EQ_PRIMARY	COUNTRY	TOTAL_DEATHS	FLAG_TSUNAMI	FOCAL_DEPTH	EQ_MAG_MW	EQ_MAG_MS	INTENSITY
2909	1920-09-20 00:00:00	14	7.8	NEW CALEDONIA		Yes	35	7.8	7.9	
2910	1920-11-26 00:00:00	8	6.2	ALBANIA	200	No	25	6.2		11
2911	1920-12-16 00:00:00	12	8.3	CHINA	200000	Yes	25	8.3	8.6	12
2912	1920-12-17 00:00:00	18	6	ARGENTINA	400	No	10		6	8
2913	1920-12-18 00:00:00	2	5.6	ALBANIA		Yes			5.6	9

Subsets

What if we want to access a row, column or a value inside the DataFrame. For this purpose, Loc, iLos, iat and at are devised. Loc and iLoc have a slight difference. If columns or rows are going to be selected by name, then Loc would be a proper choice. But if the selection is due to the index number of the row/column iLoc ought to be employed.

Syntax:
df.loc[rows label, columns label]
df.iloc[rows index, columns index]
df.iat[row, column]

In
```
print(df.loc[2909:2915, ['COUNTRY', 'FOCAL_DEPTH']])
```

54

Chapter 3

Out

	COUNTRY	FOCAL_DEPTH
2909	NEW CALEDONIA	35
2910	ALBANIA	25
2911	CHINA	25
2912	ARGENTINA	10
2913	ALBANIA	
2914	ITALY	
2915	GUATEMALA	120

In

```
print(df.iloc[0:7, [3,6]])
```

Out

	COUNTRY	FOCAL_DEPTH
2909	NEW CALEDONIA	35
2910	ALBANIA	25
2911	CHINA	25
2912	ARGENTINA	10
2913	ALBANIA	
2914	ITALY	
2915	GUATEMALA	120

Obviously both outputs are the same; however, the method of reaching to the results is dependent on whether a user uses `iloc` or `loc`.

`iat` is useful when the aim is returning a single value from a DataFrame.

Summarize data

When general characteristics of a DataFrame are needed, summarizing methods could be really helpful.

`Value-counts()`: count the number of rows with unique value of a variable.

`Len (df)`: number of rows in a DataFrame.

`Df.shape` : a tuple showa ing number of rows and columns.

`Df.describe()`: basic statistics for each column.

Chapter 3

In
```
print(df.shape)
```

Out
(3280, 10)
This means the DataFrame consists of 3280 rows and 10 columns.

In
```
print(len(df))
```

Out
3280
This output demonstrates the total number of rows.

In
```
print(df.describe())
```

Chapter 3

Out

	HOUR	EQ_PRIMARY	TOTAL_DEATHS	FOCAL_DEPTH	EQ_MAG_MW	EQ_MAG_MS	INTENSITY
count	3159	3061	1146	2774	1264	1945	1267
mean	11.33618	6.275008	1934.882	38.3248	6.470174	6.402365	7.550908
std	7.069298	1.040462	16520.45	67.00808	0.914511	0.9866	1.968846
min	0	1.6	1	0	3.6	2.1	2
25%	5	5.5	2	10	5.7	5.6	6
50%	11	6.3	7	24	6.4	6.5	8
75%	18	7.1	51.75	36	7.2	7.2	9
max	23	9.5	316000	675	9.5	9.1	12

Each of the following summary functions returns a pandas series for each column.
`Sum()` : sum the values
`Count()` : count non-null values
`Median()` : median value
`Min()`, `max()`, `mean()`, `var()`, and `std()` return respectively, the minimum, maximum, mean, var,iance and standard deviation of each object.

New columns
1. `df.assign()` : computes and appends a new column to the DataFrame.
2. `df[' name of the new column']` = " the operation"
3. `df.apply()` : computes and appends a new column to the DataFrame

In
In the earthquake DataFrame we need to evaluate the energy released from earthquakes, but this column does not exist. So that we are going to create the new column with the respective formula which is: $\log_{10} E = 4.4 + 1.5 * M$

In this equation, E is the total released energy in J and M is the magnitude of the earthquake ionRichter scale. For this purpose, a new column should be emerged.
Method 1- assign:

Chapter 3

```
df.assign(EQ_ENERGY = lambda x: 10**(4.4+1.5*x.EQ_PRIMARY))
```

Method 2- simple new column:
```
df['EQ_ENERGY'] = 10**(4.4+1.5*df['EQ_PRIMARY'])
```

Method 3- apply:
```
def energy(x):
    return 10**(4.4+1.5*x)
df['EQ_ENERGY'] = df['EQ_PRIMARY'].apply(energy)
```

Out
First five rows with columns added

	Date	HOUR	EQ_PRIMARY	COUNTRY	TOTAL_DEATHS	FLAG_TSUNAMI	FOCAL_DEPTH	EQ_MAG_MW	EQ_MAG_MS	INTENSITY	EQ_ENERGY
2909	1920-09-20 00:00:00	14	7.8	NEW CALEDONIA		Yes	35	7.8	7.9		1.26E+16
2910	1920-11-26 00:00:00	8	6.2	ALBANIA	200	No	25	6.2		11	5.01E+13
2911	1920-12-16 00:00:00	12	8.3	CHINA	200000	Yes	25	8.3	8.6	12	7.08E+16
2912	1920-12-17 00:00:00	18	6	ARGENTINA	400	No	10		6	8	2.51E+13
2913	1920-12-18 00:00:00	2	5.6	ALBANIA		Yes			5.6	9	6.31E+12

All the outputs are pretty similar. However, `assign()` method makes a copy of the original DataFrame and does the operation on the new copy while keeping the original one intact. On the other hand, method 2 and method 3 do the operation on the main DataFrame which may affect your original data.

Chapter 3

Filtering a DataFrame
Introduction to regex:

Regular expression or regex is a combination of characters facilitating the search throughout documents, datasets, or even words. You are probably familiar with the concept of *"find"* in MSWord, where you can easily search the document for your wanted string. With this in mind, regex would be called a more powerful tool for this purpose which is not limited to words. Numbers, patterns, and thousands of combinations could be controlled via regex. Here some useful features are illustrated through examples. Here are copies, notes, books, and cheat sheets on regex that you can refer to if it is not covered here.

Regex (regular expressions) examples	
'\.'	Matches strings containing a period '.'
'Length$'	Matches strings ending with the word 'Length'
'^Sepal'	Matches strings beginning with the word 'Sepal'
'^x[1-5]$'	Matches strings beginning with 'x' and ending with 1,2,3,4,5
'^(?!Species$).*'	Matches strings except the string 'Species'

If there are a large number of data in your DataFrame, you may need to filter it to gain a better understanding of your data. For example, in a DataFrame f thousands of earthquakes, you just need magnitude and country:

Syntax:

```
DataFrame.filter(items=None, like=None, regex=None, axis=None)
```

In
```
df.filter(items=['EQ_PRIMARY','COUNTRY'])
```

Chapter 3

Out
First five rows of the filtered DataFrame

	EQ_PRIMARY	COUNTRY
2909	7.8	NEW CALEDONIA
2910	6.2	ALBANIA
2911	8.3	CHINA
2912	6	ARGENTINA
2913	5.6	ALBANIA

Sorting

Unlike filtering, in sorting methods, the argument is not necessarily an index. For example, in our DataFrame, name is not an index but it is one of the consisting elements of the DataFrame. With sorting we could access to all names which are "ARGENTINA" and consequent family names and addresses. Or in the very DataFrame we aim to sort the magnitude of earthquakes in a descending order.

```
Syantax:

DataFrame, sort-values (by, axis=0, asending= True, inplace=
False, kind= 'quicksort', na-positions=' last', ignore-index=
False, key=none)
```

Chapter 3

In
```
df.sort_values(by=['EQ_PRIMARY'], axis=0,ascending=False)
```

Out
First five rows of sorted DataFrame

	Date	HOUR	EQ_PRIMARY	COUNTRY	TOTAL_DEATHS	FLAG_TSUNAMI	FOCAL_DEPTH	EQ_MAG_MW	EQ_MAG_MS	INTENSITY	EQ_ENERGY
3792	1960-05-22 00:00:00	19	9.5	CHILE	2226	Yes	33	9.5	8.5	12	4.47E+18
3904	1964-03-28 00:00:00	3	9.2	USA	139	Yes	33	9.2	8.4	10	1.58E+18
5284	2004-12-26 00:00:00	0	9.1	INDONESIA	227899	Yes	30	9.1	8.8		1.12E+18
5684	2011-03-11 00:00:00	5	9.1	JAPAN	18431	Yes	30	9.1	8.3		1.12E+18
3608	1952-11-04 00:00:00	16	9	RUSSIA	10000	Yes	22	9	8.5	7	7.94E+17

Groupby
This is used for grouping data according to the categories and collecting data more efficient.
```
syntax:
      DataFrame.groupby(by=None, axis=0)
```

61

Chapter 3

In

```
df_country = df.groupby(['COUNTRY','date'])
print(df_country.first())
```

Out

```
                            date    HOUR   EQ_PRIMARY  TOTAL_DEATHS  ...  EQ_MAG_MS  INTENSITY    EQ_ENERGY
COUNTRY                                                              ...
AFGHANISTAN           1921-11-15   20.0          7.8           NaN  ...        NaN        NaN   1.258925e+16
                      1922-12-06   13.0          7.5           NaN  ...        NaN        NaN   4.466836e+15
                      1929-02-01   17.0          7.1           NaN  ...        NaN        NaN   1.122018e+15
                      1937-11-14   10.0          7.2           NaN  ...        7.2        7.0   1.584893e+15
                      1939-11-21   11.0          6.9           NaN  ...        NaN        NaN   5.623413e+14
...                          ...    ...          ...           ...  ...        ...        ...            ...
WALLIS AND FUTUNA     1993-03-12   14.0          6.4           5.0  ...        6.4        NaN   1.000000e+14
YEMEN                 1941-01-11    8.0          5.9        1200.0  ...        5.9        8.0   1.778279e+13
                      1982-12-13    9.0          6.0        2800.0  ...        6.0        8.0   2.511886e+13
                      1991-11-22    0.0          4.7          11.0  ...        NaN        NaN   2.818383e+11
ZAMBIA                2017-02-24    0.0          5.9           NaN  ...        NaN        NaN   1.778279e+13
```

In this example, you can see that based on countries and date, information is shown.

Mini project

In this mini project, we have two types of sections including box and pipe for which we have to calculate some geometrical properties. These properties include area, center of gravity, moment of inertia for both axes, and plastic section module.

In

Line1-Line3: import required libraries

Line-Line9: create a DataFrame from a dictionary made up of `section_type_pipe` and `pipes_diameter`

Line12: defines a function to calculate the area of the section

Line16: defines a function to calculate the moment of inertia of the section

Line20: defines a function to calculate the plastic module of the section

Line24-Line27: utilize functions defined in line12,16 and 20 to add related columns into the DataFrame

Line28: rounds the values in the DataFrame with 2 decimals

Line31-Line59: repeats all the aforementioned steps for the box section

Line62-Line68: change values in columns of both DataFrames to distinguished lists

Chapter 3

Line70-Line73: make a dictionary from lists organized in line62-line68 and eventually creates the final DataFrame

```python
import pandas as pd
import numpy as np
import math
section_type_pipes = ['pipe', 'pipe', 'pipe', 'pipe']
pipes_diameter = [20, 30, 40, 50]
thickness_pipes = [2, 3, 4, 3]
dict_pipes = {'section': section_type_pipes,
              'diameter(mm)': pipes_diameter, 'thickness(mm)': thickness_pipes}
df = pd.DataFrame(dict_pipes)


def cross_area_pipes(d, t):
    return (math.pi*(d**2)/4) - math.pi*((d-2*t)**2)/4


def moment_inertia(d, t):
    return math.pi*(d**4-(d-2*t)**4)/64


def module_plastic_pipes(d, t):
    return 1.333*(d**3-(d-2*t)**3)


df['cross_area'] = cross_area_pipes(df['diameter(mm)'], df['thickness(mm)'])
df['Ixx'] = moment_inertia(df['diameter(mm)'], df['thickness(mm)'])
df['Iyy'] = moment_inertia(df['diameter(mm)'], df['thickness(mm)'])
df['Zp'] = module_plastic_pipes(df['diameter(mm)'], df['thickness(mm)'])
df = df.round(2)
print(df)

section_type_box = ['box', 'box', 'box', 'box']
box_section_length = [20, 30, 40, 50]
thickness_box = [2, 3, 4, 3]
dict_box = {'section': section_type_box,
            'length(mm)': box_section_length, 'thickness(mm)': thickness_box}
df_box = pd.DataFrame(dict_box)


def cross_area_box(l, t):
    return l**2-(l-2*t)**2


def moment_inertia_box(l, t):
    return l**4/12-(l-2*t)**4/12


def module_plastic_box(l, t):
```

63

```python
48)    return (l**4/12-(l-2*t)**4/12)/(6*l)
49)
50)
51)df_box['cross_area'] = cross_area_box(
52)    df_box['length(mm)'], df_box['thickness(mm)'])
53)df_box['Ixx'] = moment_inertia_box(
54)    df_box['length(mm)'], df_box['thickness(mm)'])
55)df_box['Iyy'] = moment_inertia_box(
56)    df_box['length(mm)'], df_box['thickness(mm)'])
57)df_box['Zp'] = module_plastic_box(
58)    df_box['length(mm)'], df_box['thickness(mm)'])
59)df_box = df_box.round(2)
60)print(df_box)
61)
62)dimension_list = df["diameter(mm)"].tolist()+df_box['length(mm)'].tolist()
63)section_list = df["section"].tolist()+df_box['section'].tolist()
64)thickness_list = df["thickness(mm)"].tolist()+df_box['thickness(mm)'].tolist()
65)cross_area_list = df["cross_area"].tolist()+df_box['cross_area'].tolist()
66)moment_x_list = df["Ixx"].tolist()+df_box['Ixx'].tolist()
67)moment_y_list = df["Iyy"].tolist()+df_box['Iyy'].tolist()
68)zp_list = df["Zp"].tolist()+df_box['Zp'].tolist()
69)
70)dict_elements = {'section': section_list,
71)                 'dimension(mm)': dimension_list, 'thickness(mm)': thickness_list,
72)                 'Ixx': moment_x_list, 'Iyy': moment_y_list, 'plastic_module': zp_list}
73)df_final = pd.DataFrame(dict_elements)
74)print(df_final)
75)
```

Chapter 3

Out

section	diameter(mm)	thickness(mm)	cross_area	Ixx	Iyy	Zp
pipe	20	2	113.1	4636.99	4636.99	5204.03
pipe	30	3	254.47	23474.77	23474.77	17563.61
pipe	40	4	452.39	74191.85	74191.85	41632.26
pipe	50	3	442.96	122811.93	122811.93	53074.73

section	length(mm)	thickness(mm)	ross_area	Ixx	Iyy	Zp
box	20	2	144	7872.0	7872.0	65.60
box	30	3	324	39852.0	39852.0	221.40
box	40	4	576	125952.0	125952.0	524.80
box	50	3	564	208492.0	208492.0	694.97

section	dimension(mm)	thickness(mm)	Ixx	Iyy	plastic_module
pipe	20	2	4636.99	4636.99	5204.03
pipe	30	3	23474.77	23474.77	17563.61
pipe	40	4	74191.85	74191.85	41632.26
pipe	50	3	122811.9	122811.93	53074.73
box	20	2	7872	7872.00	65.60
box	30	3	39852	39852.00	221.40
box	40	4	125952	125952.00	524.80
box	50	3	208492	208492.00	694.97

Chapter 4
Matplotlib

In this chapter, a general overview of drawing a graph will be discussed and in the examples, if a new command pops out, the syntax will be represented. So it is recommended to learn the overview and follow the examples meticulously.

Creating a figure and a set of subplots
```
Syntax:
 plt.subplots()
```

Plotting y versus x as lines and/or markers
Syntax

```
ax.plot(x, y,color='green',marker='o',linestyle='dashed',
    linewidth=2, markersize=12)
```

Chapter 4

NB: value for color, marker and linestyle are brought in right after the examples.
NB: given the graph type, ax.plot could change (more details in the upcoming examples)

Setting the title

Syntax:
```
Ax.set_title('title of the graph')
```

Setting x and y axis label
syntax:
```
Ax.set_xlabel('name of the axis', loc=**)
** 'left', 'center', 'right'
```

NB: this works for the x-axis if you want to name the y axis just put y instead of x

Generating the legend
syntax:
```
ax.legend()
```

Saving the graph in the desired format

syntax:
```
savefig(fname, *, dpi=*, format=**)
```

*: The resolution is dots per inch. If 'figure', use the figure's dpi value
**: The file format, e.g. 'png', 'pdf', 'svg'.

These are necessary steps toward making a graph although some extra parameters exist and some of them will be discussed in the examples. Advanced parameters' documents could be found at https://matplotlib.org.

Chapter 4

Example 1
Create a simple graph with values in the table below.

Axis	Values	Label	Graph title	save format
X	[0,11)	X(unit)	Simple graph	jpeg
Y	$y = 2x^2 +1$	Y(unit)		

Line1-Line3: import the required libraries
Line5-Line7: line 5 generates arrays from 1 to 11
Line 6 generates a function. $y = 2x^2 +1$
Line8-Line16: exactly like the general overview
NB: line9-line10: `ls` is the shorthand for `linestyle`

In
```
line1 : import numpy as np
line2 : import pandas as pd
line3 : import matplotlib.pyplot as plt
line4 :
line5 : x = np.arange(0, 11, 1)
line6 : y = 2*(x**2)+1
line7 : z = x**3-2
line8 : fig, ax = plt.subplots()
line9 : ax.plot(x, y, label='polynomial', ls=":", color='green',
line10:         marker='o', linewidth=2, markersize=8)
line11: ax.set_title('simple graph')
line12: ax.set_xlabel('x(unit)', loc='right')
line13: ax.set_ylabel('y(unit)', loc='center')
line14: ax.legend()
line15: fig.savefig('1.jpeg')
line16: plt.show()
```

Out

Chapter 4

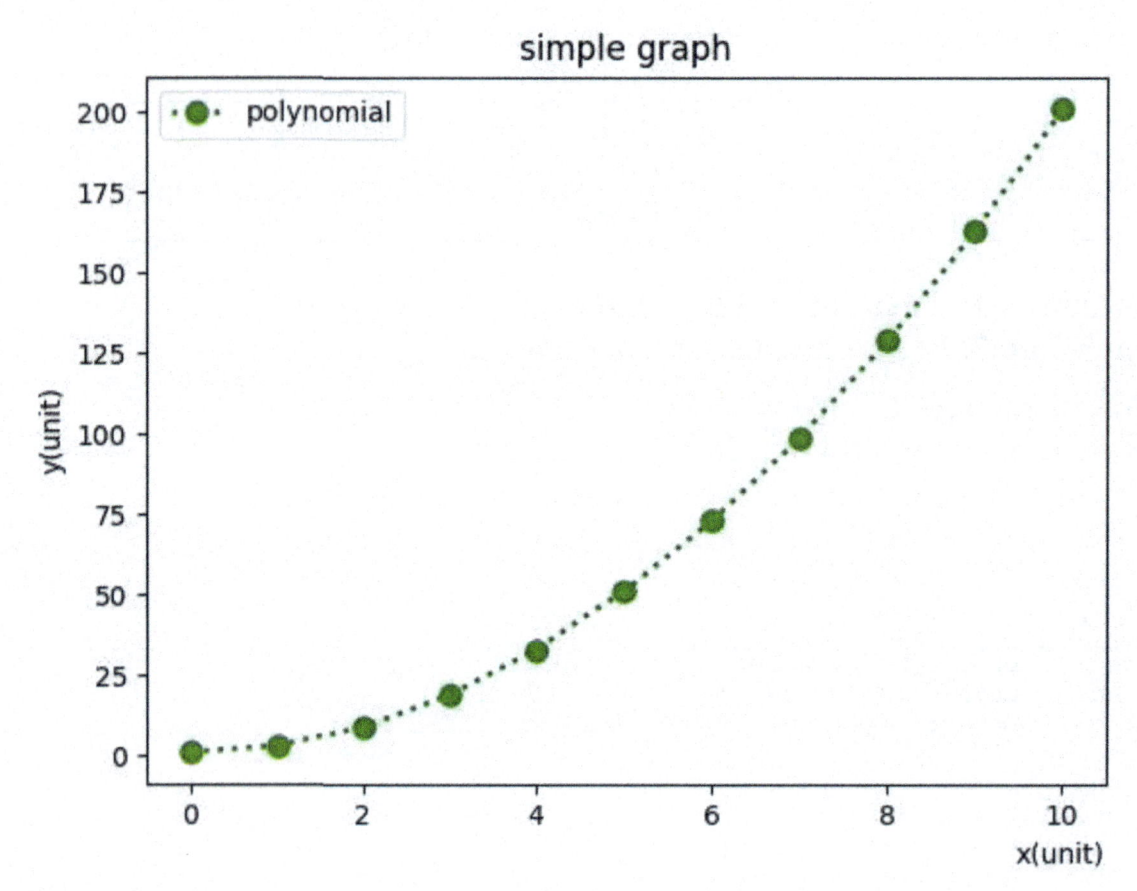

simple graph

Example2
Creates a bar chart with the following criteria.

Axis	values	Label	Width of bars	Graph title	Legend type
X	[0,11)	X(unit)	0.25	Simple graph	Arbitrary names
Y	$2x^2+1, x^3-2$	Y(unit)			

Line1-Line3: import the required libraries
Line5-Line7: line 5 generates arrays from 1 to 11
Line 6 generates a function. $y = 2x^2 +1$
Line 7 generates a function. $y = x^3 - 2$
Line8-Line15: the procedure of drawing the graph (see the general overview)

69

Chapter 4

NB: line9: `ax.bar()` is used for creating a bar chart. Plus, width of columns are determined as 0.25.

NB: line10: shifts the location of x values to the right by 0.25(the location of orange bars)

NB: line14: forces the graph to use 'legend1' and 'legend2' for legends

In

```
line1 : import numpy as np
line2 : import pandas as pd
line3 : import matplotlib.pyplot as plt
line4 :
line5 : x = np.arange(0, 11, 1)
line6 : y = 2*(x**2)+1
line7 : z = x**3-2
line8 : fig, ax = plt.subplots()
line9 : ax.bar(x, y, width=0.25)
line10: ax.bar(x+0.25, z, width=0.25)
line11: ax.set_title('simple graph')
line12: ax.set_xlabel('x(unit)', loc='right')
line13: ax.set_ylabel('y(unit)', loc='center')
line14: ax.legend(labels=['legend1', 'legend2'])
line15: plt.show()
```

Chapter 4

Out

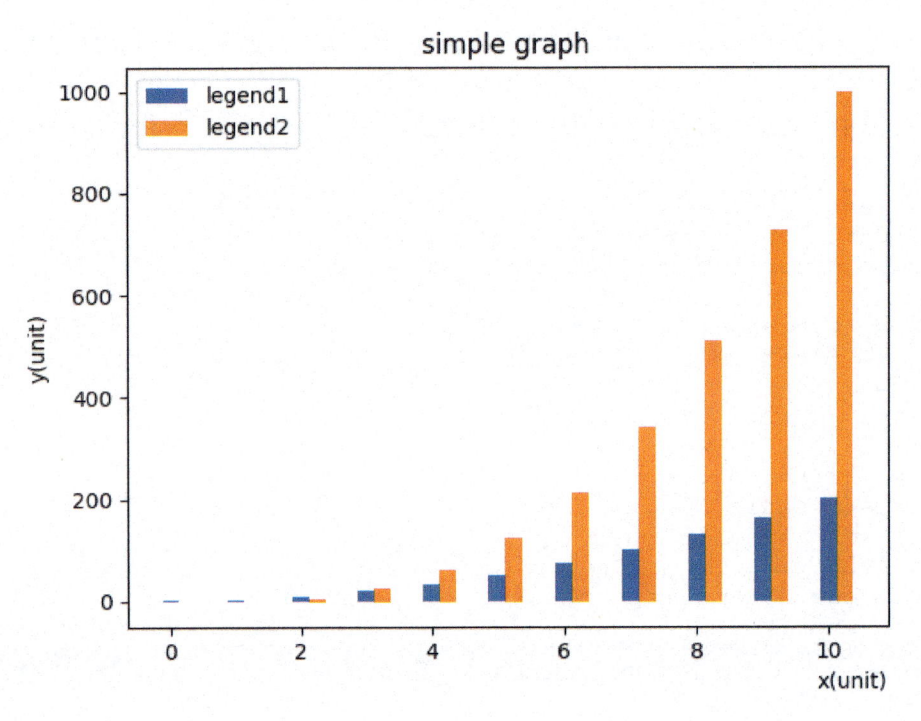

simple graph

[Bar chart showing two series (legend1 in blue, legend2 in orange) with x(unit) from 0 to 10 and y(unit) from 0 to 1000]

Example3

Creates multiple graphs

Line1-Line3: import the required libraries

Line4-Line6: line 4 generates arrays from 1 to 11

Line 5 generates a function. $y = 2x^2 + 1$

Line 6 generates a function. $y = x^3 - 2$

Line7-Line22: the procedure of drawing the graph (see the general overview)

NB: Line7: `plt.subplots(2,2)` makes it clear to python that four graphs are going to be created. If one wants 9 graphs, just change the (2,2) to (3,3) which means 3 graphs in rows and 3 graphs in columns

NB: Line7: fig, `ax` should change to `fig, axs` since we have more than one graph

NB: Line8-Line15: given the coordination we write as a tuple; the related graph's parameters are set.

NB: Line18-Line19: this brings values in horizontal and vertical axis

71

Chapter 4

In

```
line1 : import numpy as np
line2 : import pandas as pd
line3 : import matplotlib.pyplot as plt
line4 : x = np.arange(0, 11, 1)
line5 : y = 2*(x**2)+1
line6 : z = x**3-2
line7 : fig, axs = plt.subplots(2, 2)
line8 : axs[0, 0].plot(x, y, label='polynomial deg2', ls=":",
line9 :              color='green', marker='o', linewidth=2, markersize=8)
line10: axs[0, 1].plot(x, z, label='polynomial deg3', ls="-",
line11:              color='red', marker='o', linewidth=2, markersize=8)
line12: axs[1, 0].plot(x, z, label='polynomial deg3', ls="--",
line13:              color='blue', marker='o', linewidth=2, markersize=8)
line14: axs[1, 1].plot(x, z, label='polynomial deg3', ls="-.",
line15:              color='black', marker='o', linewidth=2, markersize=8)
line16: fig.suptitle('simple graph')
line17: fig.legend()
line18: for ax in axs.flat:
line19:     ax.set(xlabel='x-label', ylabel='y-label')
line20: # for ax in axs.flat:
line21: #     ax.label_outer()
line22: plt.show()
```

Chapter 4

Out

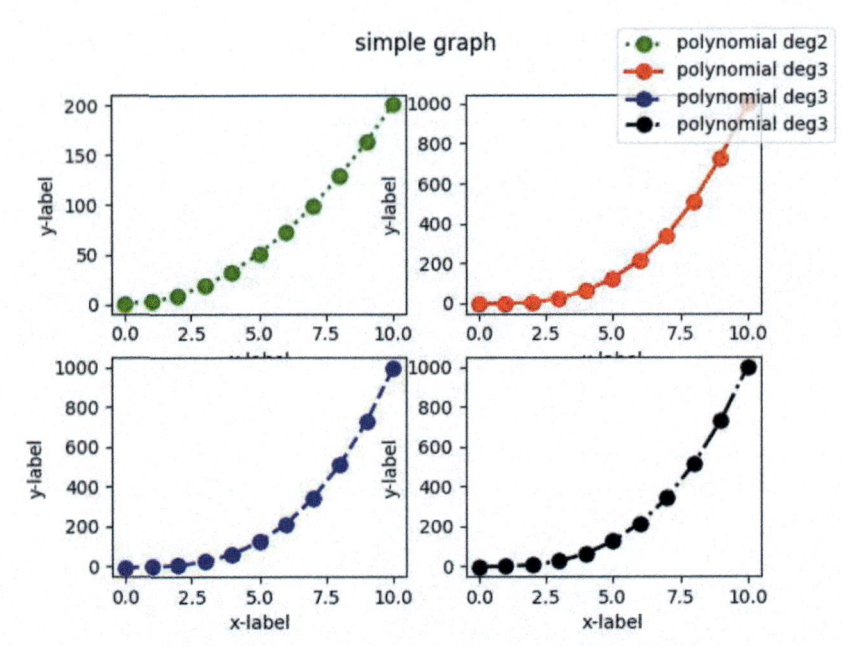

NB: Line20-Line21: if we uncomment them, the final picture will be like:

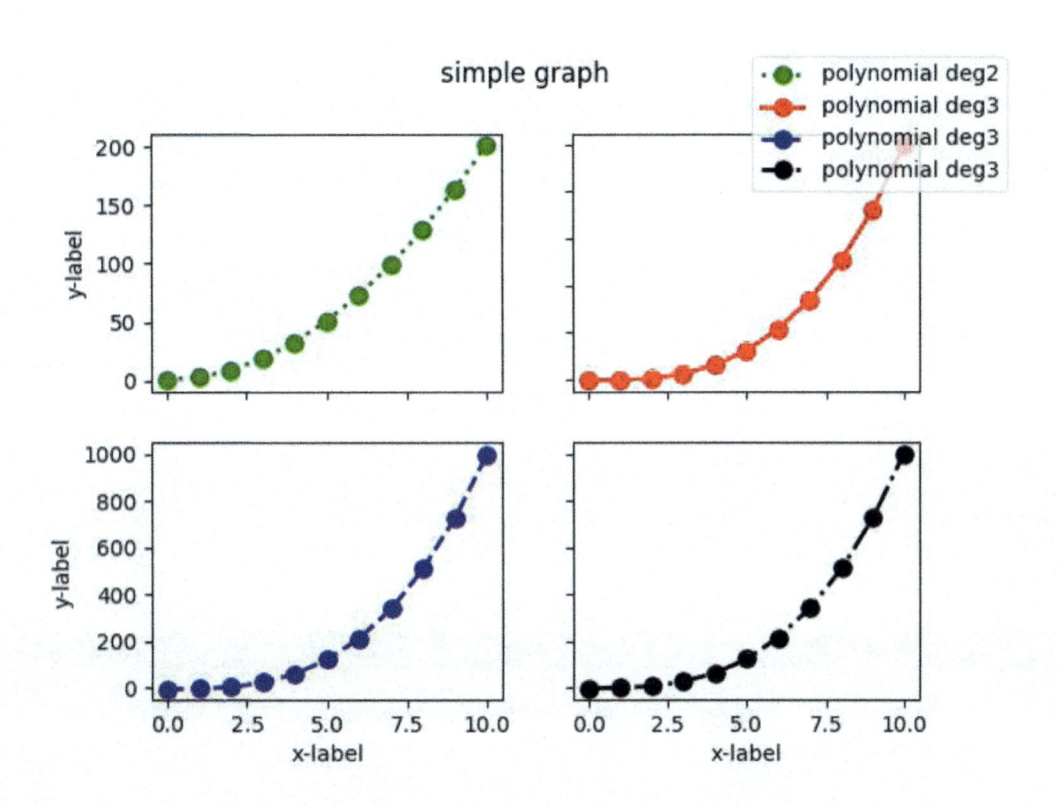

Example4

Creates two graphs next to each other
Line1-Line3: import the required libraries
Line4-Line6: line 4 generates arrays from 1 to 11

Line 5 generates a function. $y = 2x^2 + 1$

Line 6 generates a function. $y = x^3 - 2$

Line7-Line22: the procedure of drawing the graph (see the general overview)

NB: **Line7:** fig, `(ax1, ax2)=plt.subplots(1,2)` which means two graphs in a row

NB: **Line8, Line10:** Each ax should be dealt with separately
Rest is like the general overview
In

Chapter 4

```python
line1 : import numpy as np
line2 : import pandas as pd
line3 : import matplotlib.pyplot as plt
line4 : x = np.arange(0, 11, 1)
line5 : y = 2*(x**2)+1
line6 : z = x**3-2
line7 : fig, (ax1, ax2) = plt.subplots(1, 2)
line8 : ax1.plot(x, y, label='polynomial deg2', ls=":",
line9 :          color='green', marker='o', linewidth=2, markersize=8)
line10: ax2.plot(x, z, label='polynomial deg3', ls=":",
line11:          color='green', marker='o', linewidth=2, markersize=8)
line12: fig.suptitle('simple graph')
line13: ax1.set_xlabel('x(unit)', loc='right')
line14: ax1.set_ylabel('y(unit)', loc='top')
line15: ax2.set_xlabel('x(unit)', loc='right')
line16: ax2.set_ylabel('y(unit)', loc='top')
line17: fig.legend()
line18: plt.show()
```

Chapter 4

Out

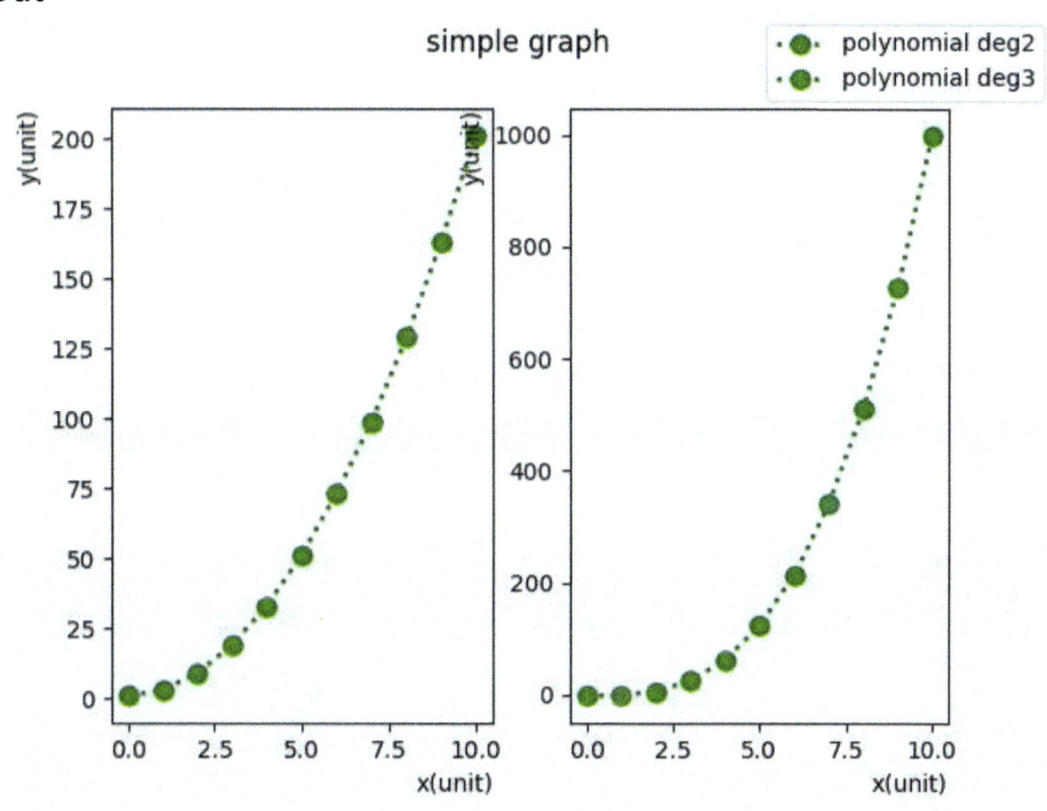

Example5
Creates two graphs vertically positioned
Line1-Line3: import the required libraries
Line4-Line6: line 4 generates arrays from 1 to 11

Line 5 generates a function. $y = 2x^2 + 1$

Line 6 generates a function. $y = x^3 - 2$

Line7-Line15: the procedure of drawing the graph (see the general overview)
 NB: line7: fig, `(ax1, ax2)= plt.subplots(2)` which means two graphs placed vertically. Each ax should be dealt with separately
 Rest is like the general overview

76

Chapter 4

```
line1 :import numpy as np
line2 :import pandas as pd
line3 :import matplotlib.pyplot as plt
line4 :x = np.arange(0, 11, 1)
line5 :y = 2*(x**2)+1
line6 :z = x**3-2
line7 :fig, ax = plt.subplots(2)
line8 :ax[0].plot(x, y, label='polynomial deg2', ls=":",
line9 :          color='green', marker='o', linewidth=2, markersize=8)
line10:ax[1].plot(x, z, label='polynomial deg3', ls=":",
line11:          color='green', marker='o', linewidth=2, markersize=8)
line12:fig.suptitle('simple graph')
line13:ax[1].set_xlabel('x(unit)', loc='right')
line14:fig.legend()
line15:plt.show()
```

Chapter 4

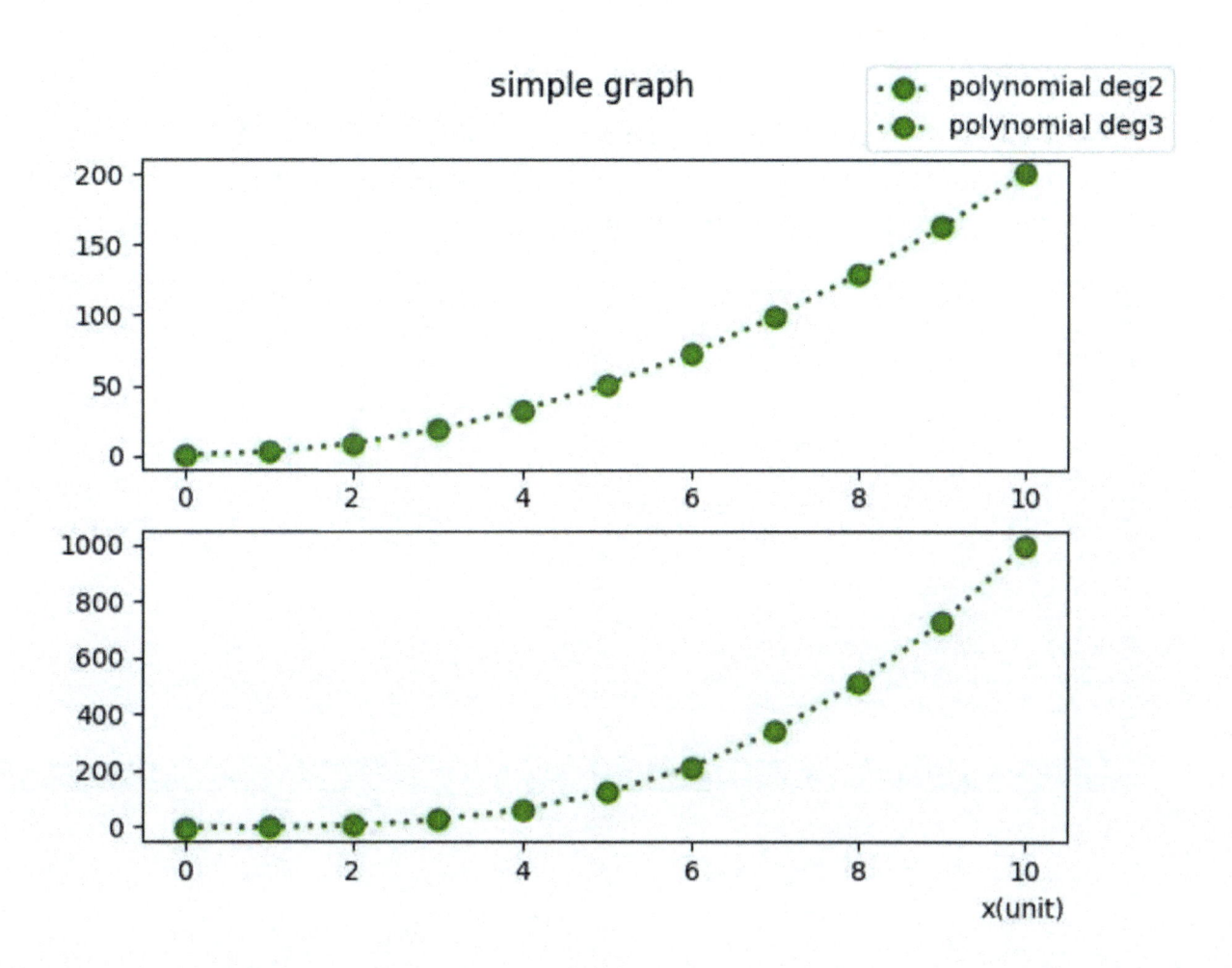

Example6
Create a scatter graph

Axis	values	Label	Graph title	save format
X	[0,11)	X(unit)	Simple graph	jpeg
Y	$y = 2x^2 + 1$	Y(unit)		

Line1-Line3: import the required libraries
Line5-Line7: line 5 generates arrays from 1 to 11

78

Chapter 4

Line 6 generates a function. $y = 2x^2 + 1$

Line8-Line16: exactly like the general overview

NB: line9-line10: instead of `plt.plot()` we use `plt.scatter()` to draw a scatter graph. Rest is like previous examples

```
line1 : import numpy as np
line2 : import pandas as pd
line3 : import matplotlib.pyplot as plt
line4 :
line5 : x = np.arange(0, 11, 1)
line6 : y = 2*(x**2)+1
line7 : z = x**3-2
line8 : fig, ax = plt.subplots()
line9 : ax.scatter(x, y, label='polynomial', ls="-", color='green',
line10:           marker='p', linewidth=2)
line11: ax.set_title('simple graph')
line12: ax.set_xlabel('x(unit)', loc='right')
line13: ax.set_ylabel('y(unit)', loc='center')
line14: ax.legend()
line15: plt.show()
```

Chapter 4

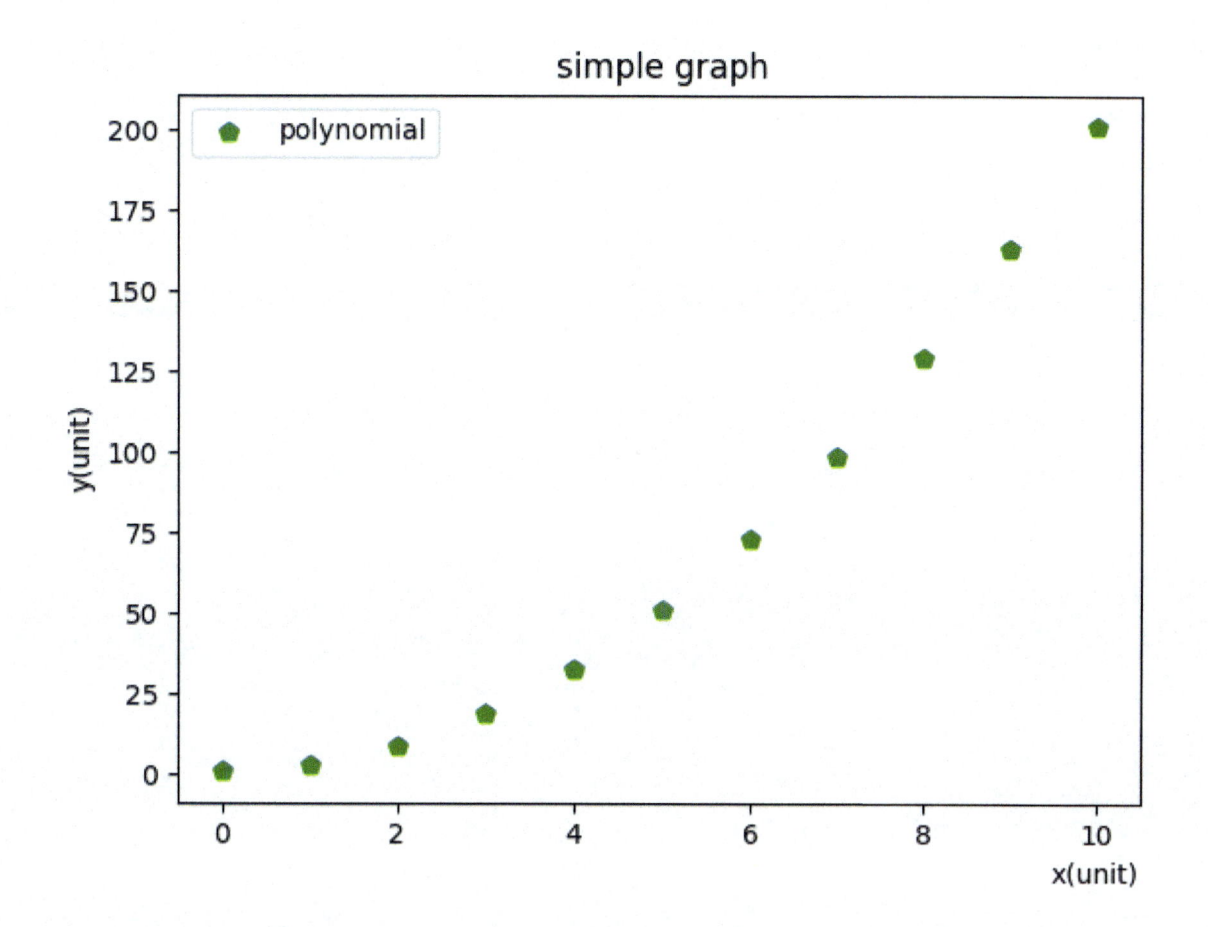

Example7
Create a pie chart with below percentages

labels	Percentage
A	15
B	30
C	45
D	10

This is pretty simple. We just use the `ax.pie()`

Chapter 4

```python
import matplotlib.pyplot as plt
labels = 'a', 'b', 'c', 'd'
sizes = [15, 30, 45, 10]

fig, ax = plt.subplots()
ax.pie(sizes, labels=labels, autopct='%1.1f%%')
plt.show()
```

Chapter 4

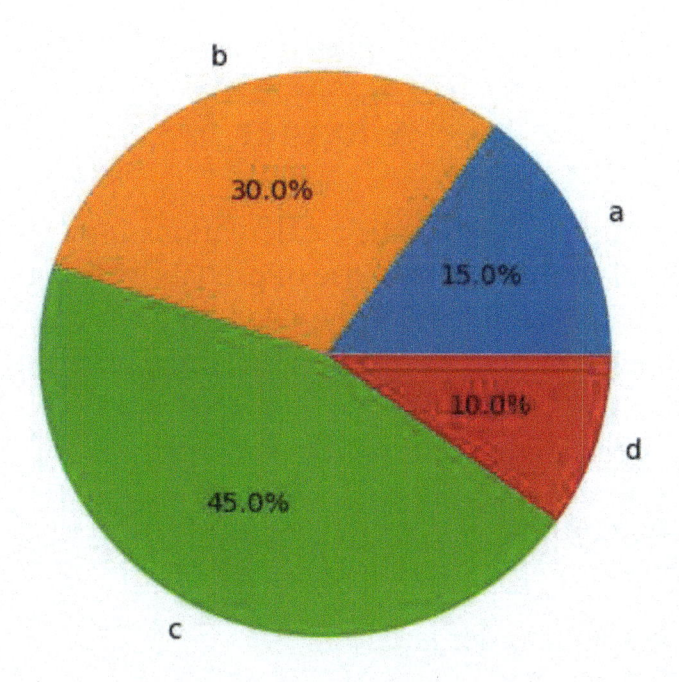

Chapter 5

Scipy

This library was designed for scientific calculations for a vast variety of realms of scince. For example, statisticians make use of probabilty functions or statistical tests. for civil engineers, given the function you need you can employ what scipy offers. However, this book aims to give an introduction on general subjects of engineering.

Derivative

This finds the nth derivative of a function at a certain point.

Syntax:
```
scipy.misc.derivative(func, x0, dx=1.0, n=1, order=**)
```

NB**: default value for the order is 1.

In
```python
from scipy.misc import derivative


def f(x):
    return x**4 + 2*x**2


print(derivative(f, 1.0, dx=1e-05))
```

Out
8.000000000407681

Chapter 5

Integration

Method	Purpose	Mathematics sign
Quad	General purpose integration.	$\int f(x)dx$
Dblquad	General purpose double integration	$\iint f(x)g(y)d(x)d(y)$
Tplquad	General purpose triple integration	$\iiint f(x)g(y)p(z)d(x)d(y)d(z)$

Syntax:
```
scipy.integrate.quad(func, x0, x1)
```

NB: if double or triple integration is used, additional pairs of boundries should be added

In

Calculate the following integrations.

		boundries	
Mathematics sign	x	y	z
$\int (3x^2 + x^2)dx$	(0,4)	----	----
$\iint (3x^2 + xy)d(x)d(y)$	(0,2)	(4,5)	----
$\iiint (3x^2 + xyz)d(x)d(y)d(z)$	(0,2)	(4,5)	(2,5)

Chapter 5

```
line1 : from scipy import integrate
line2 :
line3 : def func_1(x):
line4 :     return 3*x**2+x**2
line5 :
line6 : def func_2(x, y):
line7 :     return 3*x**2+x**y
line8 :
line9 : def func_3(x, y, z):
line10:     return 3*x**2+x**y*z
line11:
line12: print(integrate.quad(func_1, 0, 4))
line13: print(integrate.dblquad(func_2, 0, 2, 4, 5))
line14: print(integrate.tplquad(func_3, 0, 2, 4, 5, 2, 5))
```

Out

(85.33333333333334, 9.473903143468003e-13)

(134.8210688520892, 1.4968145484416297e-12)

(2983.644023703548, 5.858097829254521e-11)

Interpolation
Scipy.interpolate.interp1d

syntax

```
scipy.interpolate.interp1d(x, y, kind='linear', axis=-1, copy=True, bounds_error=None, fill_value=nan, assume_sorted=False)
```

In

Line1-Line3: import required libraries.
Line4-Line5: defines x, y as real values.
Line6: approximates the function to x, y.

85

Line7: new values are defined for x to check the function calculated in line6.
Line8: respective values for new x are calculated.
Line9: prints the values for new y.
Line10-Line12: create the graph.

```
line1 :import numpy as np
line2 :import matplotlib.pyplot as plt
line3 :from scipy import interpolate
line4 :x = np.arange(0, 10)
line5 :y = np.exp(-x/3.0)
line6 :f = interpolate.interp1d(x, y)
line7 :xnew = np.arange(0, 10, 3)
line8 :ynew = f(xnew)
line9 :print('interpolated values for the new inputs are{one}'
line10:        .format(one=np.round(ynew, 3)))
line11:plt.plot(x, y, 'o', xnew, ynew, '-')
line12:plt.show()
```

Chapter 5

Out
interpolated values for the new inputs are[1.   0.368 0.135 0.05]

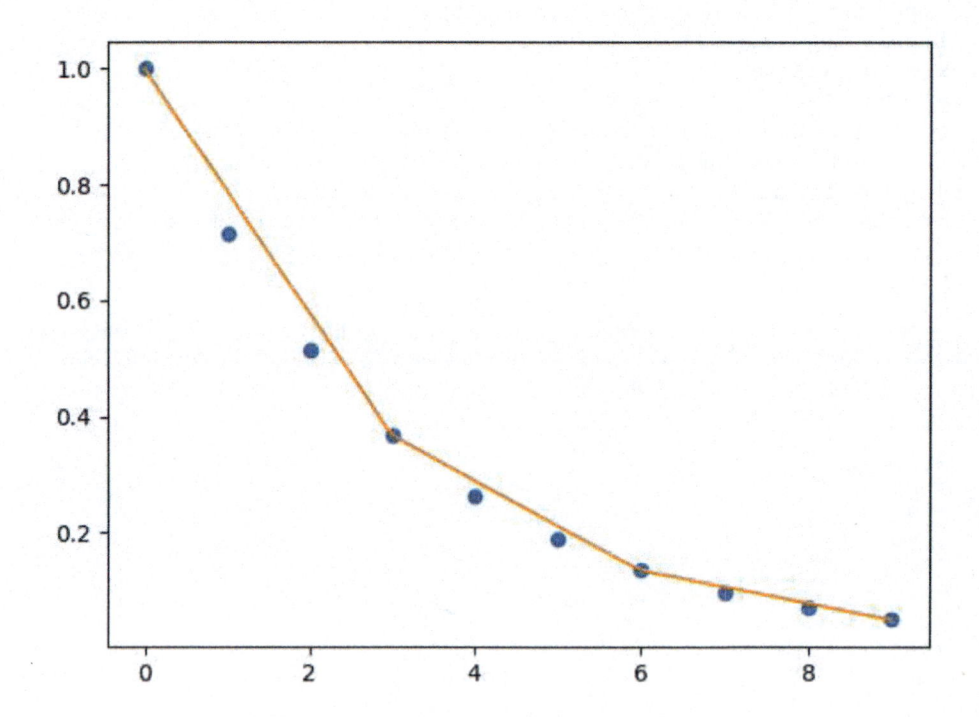

Scipy.interpolate.CubicSpline
Interpolate data with a piecewise cubic polynomial.
syntax
```
scipy.interpolate.CubicSpline(x, y, axis=0, bc_type='not-a-knot',
extrapolate=None)
```

Chapter 5

In

This example is exactly from official documents of Scipy.

Line1-Line3: import required libraries.
Line4-Line5: defines x, y as real values.
Line6: approximates the function to x, y.
Line7: new values are defined for x to check the function calculated in line6.
Line8-Line17: create the graph.

```
line1 :import numpy as np
line2 :from scipy.interpolate import CubicSpline
line3 :import matplotlib.pyplot as plt
line4 :x = np.arange(10)
line5 :y = np.sin(x)
line6 :cs = CubicSpline(x, y)
line7 :xs = np.arange(-0.5, 9.6, 0.1)
line8 :fig, ax = plt.subplots(figsize=(6.5, 4))
line9 :ax.plot(x, y, 'o', label='data')
line10:ax.plot(xs, np.sin(xs), label='true')
line11:ax.plot(xs, cs(xs), label="S")
line12:ax.plot(xs, cs(xs, 1), label="S'")
line13:ax.plot(xs, cs(xs, 2), label="S''")
line14:ax.plot(xs, cs(xs, 3), label="S'''")
line15:ax.set_xlim(-0.5, 9.5)
line16:ax.legend(loc='lower left', ncol=2)
line17:plt.show()
```

Chapter 5

Out

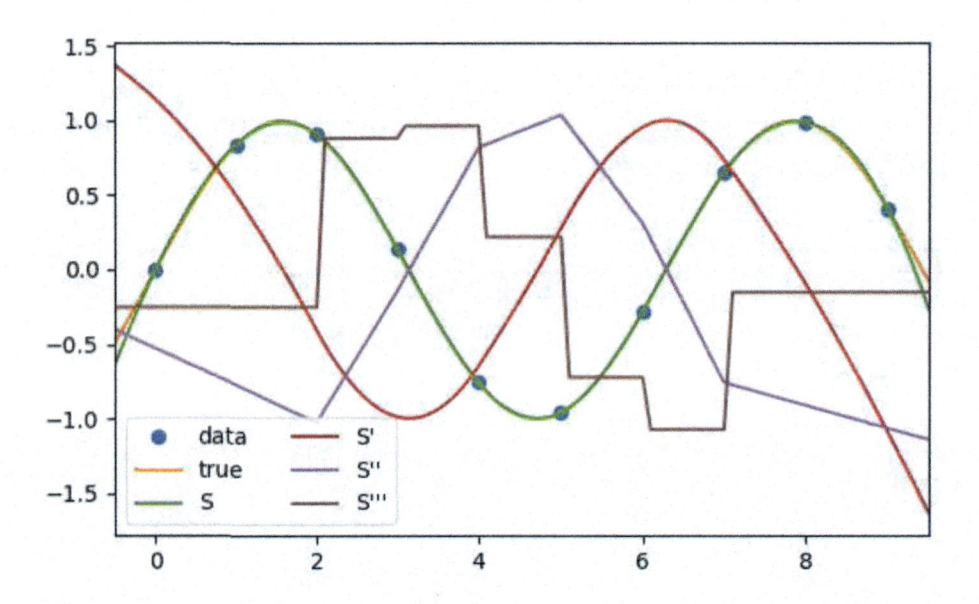

Curve fitting
Curve fitting is useful when there are points, which are often derived from experiments or analysis, and based on a defined parametric function, a curve could be fitted to the points.
In
Line1-Line3: import required libraries.
Line4-Line5: defining x and y values.
Line7-Line9: parametric function.
Line11: calculating fitted curve parameters.
NB: `Popt` here is coefficients of the defined function.

89

Chapter 5

```
line1 : from scipy.optimize import curve_fit
line2 : import numpy as np
line3 : import matplotlib.pyplot as plt
line4 : x = np.linspace(0, 100, 50)
line5 : y = x**2+x+np.random.randint(10)
line6 :
line7 : def func_1(x, a, b):
line8 :
line9 :     return a*x**3
line10:
line11: popt, pcov = curve_fit(func_1, x, y)
line12: print(popt)
```

Out
[0.01168 1.   ]

Root finding
This method finds the root of a scalar function.
Syntax
```
scipy.optimize.root_scalar(f, method=None, bracket=None)
```

NB: There are different solvers for method argument and you can find out more at https://docs.scipy.org.

In
Line1: Imports the library.
Line4-Line6: Defines the function for which we want the roots.
Line9-Line10: Defines the first derivative of the function already defined.
NB: This function is defined when Newton method is going to be applied.
Line13: Solution with `brentq` method.
NB: `bracket= [0, 3]` is optional argument which is an interval bracketing a root.
Line14: Makes use of newton method to find the roots.
NB: `fprime` is an optional argument is the first derivative of the main function with same arguments.
NB: x_0 is the initial guess and optional.

Line16-Line20: print the results.

```
line1 :from scipy import optimize
line2 :
line3 :
line4 :def f(x):
line5 :
line6 :    return (4*x**3 - 56)
line7 :
line8 :
line9 :def fprime(x):
line10:    return (12*x**2)
line11:
line12:
line13:solution_brentq = optimize.root_scalar(f, bracket=[0, 3], method='brentq')
line14:solution_newton = optimize.root_scalar(
line15:    f, x0=0.2, fprime=fprime, method='newton')
line16:print('brentq method is:')
line17:print(solution_brentq)
line18:print('*'*10)
line19:print('newotn method is:')
line20:print(solution_newton)
```

Out

brentq method is:
converged: True
flag: 'converged'
function_calls: 10
iterations: 9
root: 2.410142264175167
****

newotn method is:
converged: True
flag: 'converged'
function_calls: 30
iterations: 15
root: 2.41014226417523

Differential Equation

Differential equations could be solved by `odient` function in library Scipy.

Chapter 5

Syntax
```
odeint(model, y0, t)
```

In
Line1-Line3: Import required libraries.
Line6: Defines the following differential equations.
$$\frac{dx(t)}{dt} = 5e^{-t}$$
$$\frac{dy(t)}{dt} = 1.5 - y(t)$$
$$x(0) = 0$$
$$y(0) = 0$$

Line13: Sets the intial values.
Line14: Creates time points.
Line15: Solvees the differintal eaquations.
Line17-Line23: Depict both equations.

Chapter 5

```python
line1 :import numpy as np
line2 :from scipy.integrate import odeint
line3 :import matplotlib.pyplot as plt
line4 :
line5 :
line6 :def model(z, t):
line7 :    dxdt = 5 * np.exp(-t)
line8 :    dydt = -z[1] + 1.5
line9 :    dzdt = [dxdt, dydt]
line10:    return dzdt
line11:
line12:
line13:z0 = [0, 0]
line14:t = np.linspace(0, 5, num=35)
line15:z = odeint(model, z0, t)
line16:fig, ax = plt.subplots()
line17:ax.plot(t, z[:, 0], color='b', linestyle=':', label='equation a')
line18:ax.plot(t, z[:, 1], color='r', linestyle='dashed', label='equation b')
line19:ax.set_xlabel('response')
line20:ax.set_ylabel('time')
line21:ax.legend(loc='best')
line22:ax.grid()
line23:plt.show()
```

Chapter 5

Out

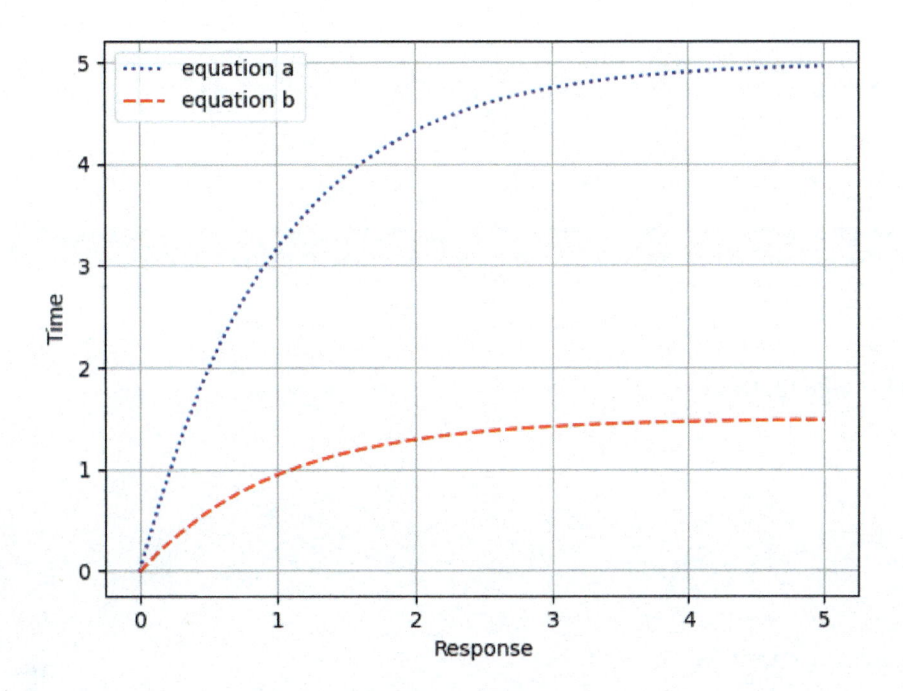

Linear Algebra

Scipy is also able to offer linear algebra operations. Here four must-learn operations will be discussed.

Linear equation

This is perhaps the most useful one in a vast variety of problems.
Syntax:
```
scipy.linalg.solve(a, b)
```

In

Line1-Line2: Import required libraries.

Line3: Defines a matrix. $\begin{pmatrix} 3 & 5 \\ 1 & 8 \end{pmatrix}$

Line4: Defines b matrix $\begin{pmatrix} 10 \\ 33 \end{pmatrix}$

Chapter 5

Line5: solves the equation.
Line6: prints the results.

```
line1:from scipy import linalg
line2:import numpy as np
line3:a = np.array([[3, 5], [1, 8]])
line4:b = np.array([10, 33])
line5:result = linalg.solve(a, b)
line6:print(result)
```

Out
[-4.47368421 4.68421053]

Inverse matrix

Syntax:
```
scipy.linalg.inv(a)
```

In

Line1-Line2: import required libraries

Line3: defines a matrix. $\begin{pmatrix} 2 & 5 \\ 12 & 8 \end{pmatrix}$

Line5: gives the invers matrix
Line6: prints the results

```
line1:from scipy import linalg
line2:import numpy as np
line3:x = np.array([[2, 5], [12, 8]])
line4:y = linalg.inv(x)
line5:print(y)
```

Out

```
[[-0.18181818  0.11363636]
 [ 0.27272727 -0.04545455]]
```

Determinant
Syntax:
```
scipy.linalg.det(a)
```

In

Line1-Line2: import required libraries.

Line3: defines a matrix. $\begin{pmatrix} 3 & 2 \\ 1 & 5 \end{pmatrix}$

Line5: calculates determinant.
Line6: prints the results.

```
line1:from scipy import linalg
line2:import numpy as np
line3:A = np.array([[3, 2], [1, 5]])
line4:D = linalg.det(A)
line5:print(D)
```

Out

13.0

Eigenvalue
Syntax:
```
scipy.linalg.eig(a)
```

In

Line1-Line2: import required libraries.

Chapter 5

Line3: defines a matrix. $\begin{pmatrix} 5 & 8 \\ 4 & 6 \end{pmatrix}$

Line4: calculates eigenvalue and its vector.
Line5-Line6: prints the results.

```
line1:from scipy import linalg
line2:import numpy as np
line3:M = np.array([[5, 8], [4, 6]])
line4:val, vect = linalg.eig(M)
line5:print(val)
line6:print(vect)
```

Out
[-0.17890835+0.j 11.17890835+0.j]
[[-0.83945347 -0.79142426]
 [0.54343157 -0.61126724]]

Mini project

In this mini project a curve fitting problem is devloped in order to find a fit or mutiple fits for x and y values. Finally, it ends up to a diagram in which different fits are shown.

In
Line1-Line3: Import required libraries.
Line4-Line5: Generate x values and y values with random noise
NB: Every time the codes strats, distinguished answers may generate.
Line8-Line45: Common curves with paramaetric values are defined

Name of the function	Equation
Linear	$a*x = b$
Quadratic	$a*x^2 + b*x + c$
Cubic	$dx^3 + ax^2 + bx + c$
quartic	$ex^4 + dx^3 + ax^2 + bx + c$

Chapter 5

quintic	$fx^5 + ex^4 + dx^3 + ax^2 + bx + c$
4pl	$d + \dfrac{(a-d)}{1+(x/c)^b}$
5pl	$d + \dfrac{(a-d)}{(1+(x/c)^b)^m}$
Exponential	$a + b\,2.71^{-cx}$
Half-life exponential	$a + \dfrac{b}{2^{\frac{x}{c}}}$
power	ax^b

Line48-Line59: Define a dictionary in which all functions are defined to be called.

Line60-Line63: If a function is called which does not exist in the dictionary, this massage pops up: `your function name is not defined yet`

Line66-Line73: Define the main function. The inputs are name of the function(from `dictionary_functions`) and x, y

NB: the main function here entitled curvefit_f, return `popt` if convergence occurs, nevertheless, this massage is shown 'sorry cannot be converged with this method'

Line78-Line81: Generate new y values with corresponding `popt`

NB: To use the respective popt for every function, this command should written; also, y valuesare are calculated automatically.
`Function_name(x,*popt)`

Line83-Line97: Generate the graphs

```
line1 :from scipy.optimize import curve_fit
line2 :import numpy as np
line3 :import matplotlib.pyplot as plt
line4 :x1 = np.arange(0, 100, 5)
line5 :y1 = 1.5*x1**4+2*x1**2+x1**3+np.random.randint(15)
line6 :
line7 :
line8 :def linear_reg(x, a, b):
line9 :    return a*x+b
line10:
line11:
line12:def quadratic_reg(x, a, b, c):
line13:    return a*(x**2)+b*x+c
line14:
```

98

Chapter 5

```python
line15:
line16:def cubic_reg(x, a, b, c, d):
line17:    return d*x**3+a*x**2+b*x+c
line18:
line19:
line20:def quartic_reg(x, a, b, c, d, e):
line21:    return e*x**4+d*x**3+a*x**2+b*x+c
line22:
line23:
line24:def quintic_reg(x, a, b, c, d, e, f):
line25:    return f*x**5+e*x**4+d*x**3+a*x**2+b*x+c
line26:
line27:
line28:def four_pl_reg(x, a, b, c, d):
line29:    return d+(a-d)/(1+(x/c)**b)
line30:
line31:
line32:def five_pl_reg(x, a, b, c, d, m):
line33:    return d+(a-d)/((1+(x/c)**b)**m)
line34:
line35:
line36:def exponential_basic(x, a, b, c):
line37:    return a+b*(2.71**(-c*x))
line38:
line39:
line40:def exponential_halflife(x, a, b, c):
line41:    return a+b/(2**(x/c))
line42:
line43:
line44:def power(x, a, b):
line45:    return a*(x**b)
line46:
line47:
line48:dictionary_functions = {
line49:    'linear': linear_reg,
line50:    'quadratic': quadratic_reg,
line51:    'cubic': cubic_reg,
line52:    'quartic': quartic_reg,
line53:    'quantic': quintic_reg,
line54:    '4pl': four_pl_reg,
line55:    '5pl': five_pl_reg,
line56:    'basicexp': exponential_basic,
line57:    'halflifeexp': exponential_halflife,
line58:    'power': power
line59:}
line60:try:
line61:    name = dictionary_functions['power']
line62:except KeyError:
line63:    raise KeyError('your function name is not defined yet')
```

```
line64:
line65:
line66:def curvefit_f(name, x, y):
line67:    try:
line68:
line69:        popt, pcov = curve_fit(name, x, y)
line70:        return popt
line71:
line72:    except RuntimeError:
line73:        raise RuntimeError('sorry cannot be converged with this method')
line74:
line75:
line76:y_new_linear = linear_reg(
line77:    x1, *curvefit_f(dictionary_functions['linear'], x1, y1))
line78:y_new_quadratic = quadratic_reg(
line79:    x1, *curvefit_f(dictionary_functions['quadratic'], x1, y1))
line80:y_new_cubic = cubic_reg(x1, *curvefit_f(dictionary_functions['cubic'], x1, y1))
line81:y_new_power = power(x1, *curvefit_f(dictionary_functions['power'], x1, y1))
line82:
line83:fig, ax = plt.subplots()
line84:ax.scatter(x1, y1, marker='*', color='cyan', label='real values')
line85:ax.plot(x1, y_new_linear, linestyle='--',
line86:        color='red', label='linear regression')
line87:ax.plot(x1, y_new_quadratic, linestyle='-',
line88:        color='blue', label='quadratic regression')
line89:ax.plot(x1, y_new_cubic, linestyle=':',
line90:        color='black', label='cubic regression')
line91:ax.plot(x1, y_new_power, linestyle='-.',
line92:        color='green', label='power regression')
line93:ax.set_xlabel('x values')
line94:ax.set_ylabel('y values')
line95:ax.legend()
line96:ax.grid()
line97:plt.show()
```

Out

As the graph illustrates, cubic and power functions have been a better a fit for the real points(in this run).

Chapter 5

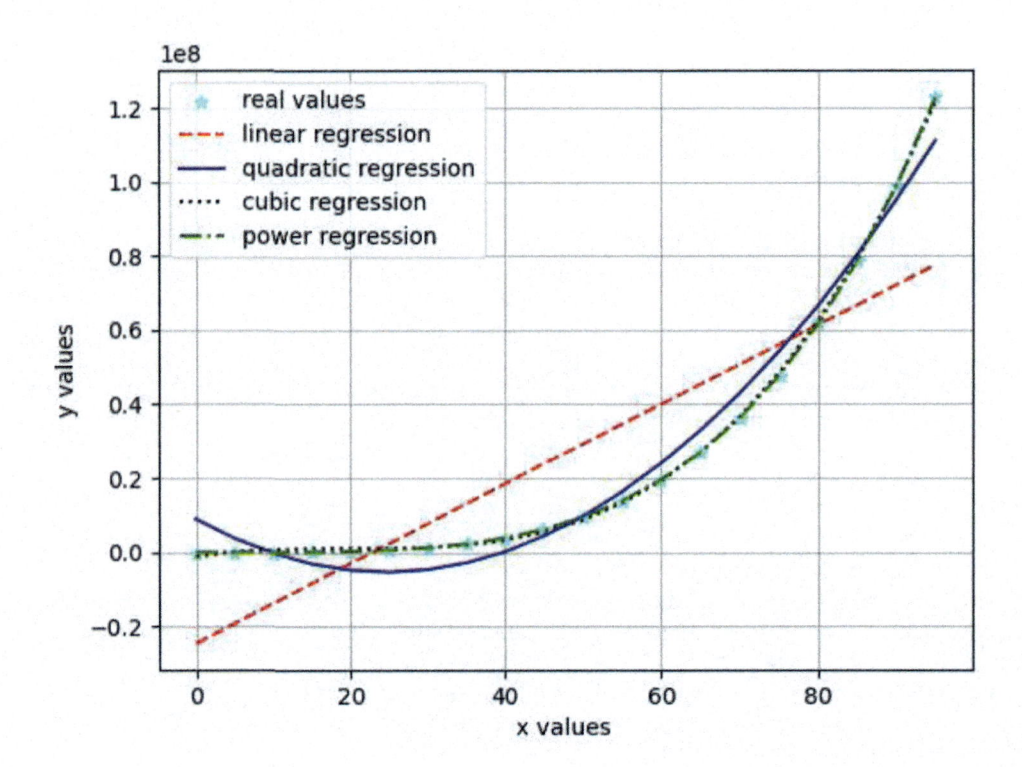

Chapter 6

Fourier series

The *Fourier series* is a representation of an arbitrary periodic function by an infinite sum of functions sin and cos multiplied by appropriate coefficients. So in other words, every periodic function could be represented with *Fourier series*.

It is used in designing electrical circuits, solving differential equations; signal processing, signal analysis, image processing & filtering. In case of civil engineering, solving differential equations would be the main reason why we might exploit the series. However, the application of Fourier series is not limited to solving ODEs[2] and PDEs[3].

The basic formulas of Fourier series are illustrated below:

$$f(t) = \frac{a_0}{2} + \sum_{n=1}^{\infty}[a_n \cos\frac{2\pi nt}{P} + b_n \sin\frac{2\pi nt}{P}]$$

$$a_0 = \frac{2}{P}\int_0^P f(t)dt$$

$$a_n = \frac{2}{P}\int_0^P f(t)\cos\frac{2\pi nt}{P}dt$$

$$b_n = \frac{2}{P}\int_0^P f(t)\sin\frac{2\pi nt}{P}dt$$

Square wave:

Let's begin our project with a well-known periodic wave called square. The general shape of this wave is like figure1.

---

[2] Ordinary differential equations (ODEs)
[3] partial differential equations (PDEs)

Chapter 6

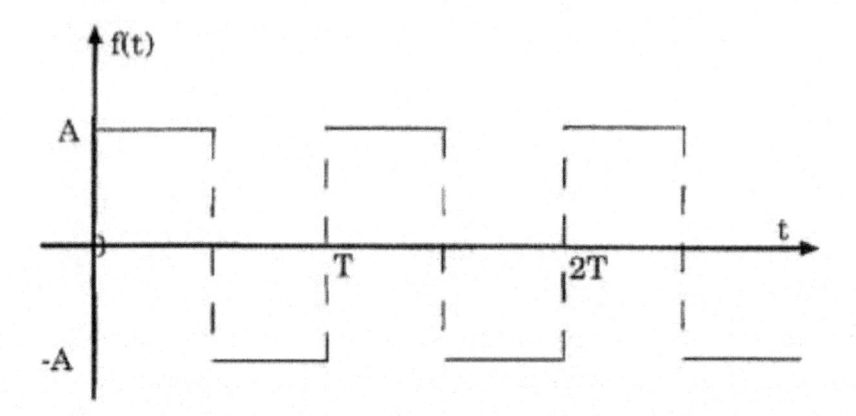

Fig.1

Firstly, we have this periodic function between 0, 1. Secondly, due to Fourier series coefficients we can estimate the function with proximity. As a rule of thumb, the more iteration (n) we bring to calculation, the less error we will have.

Now, what every line of the code is responsible is discussed.

Line1-Line5:
Line1-Line5: These lines contain the libraries we need to proceed.
Line9:
Line9: Our time period is determined.
Line15:
Line15: The wave function in the aforementioned period is defined.
Line22-Line39:

Function (here square) and number of iterations are defined.

For number of iterations Fourier series coefficients are calculated and appended to related lists.

$$a_n = \frac{2}{P}\int_0^P f(t)\cos\frac{2\pi nt}{P}dt$$

$$b_n = \frac{2}{P}\int_0^P f(t)\sin\frac{2\pi nt}{P}dt$$

The main formula is being shaped:

$$f(t) = \frac{a_0}{2} + \sum_{n=1}^{\infty}[a_n\cos\frac{2\pi nt}{P} + b_n\sin\frac{2\pi nt}{P}]$$

Fourier series coefficients and the formula value is returned

Chapter 6

Line40-Line63: There lines prepare the graph with matplotlib library.

NB: there is no absolute and determined solution for portraying the graphs. There could be more optimized way to show the graph.

```
line1 : import numpy as np
line2 : import math
line3 : from scipy.signal import square
line4 : import matplotlib.pyplot as plt
line5 : import scipy.integrate as spi
line6 : '''
line7 : time management period
line8 : '''
line9 : t = np.linspace(0, 1, 1000, endpoint=True)
line10: '''
line11: periodic function
line12: '''
line13: p = 1
line14:
line15: def f(t):
line16:     return square(2*np.pi*t)
line17:
line18: '''
line19: an , bn
line20: '''
line21:
line22: def fourier_coeffs(func, i):
line23:     a_coeff = []
line24:     b_coeff = []
line25:     for n in range(i+1):
line26:         an = (2./p) * spi.quad(lambda t: func(t) *
line27:                     np.cos(2 * np.pi * n * t / p), 0, p)[0]
line28:         bn = (2./p) * spi.quad(lambda t: func(t) *
line29:                     np.sin(2 * np.pi * n * t / p), 0, p)[0]
line30:         a_coeff.append(an)
line31:         b_coeff.append(bn)
line32:     formula = 0.5*np.array(a_coeff)[0]
line33:     for n in range(0, len(a_coeff)):
line34:         formula = formula + \
line35:             +np.array(a_coeff)[n] * np.cos(2. * np.pi * n * t / p) + \
line36:             np.array(b_coeff)[n] * np.sin(2. * np.pi * n * t / p)
line37:
line38:     return formula, a_coeff, b_coeff
line39:
line40: i = [0, 1]
line41: j = [0, 1]
line42: fig, axs = plt.subplots(2, 2)
line43: for k in i:
line44:     for z in j:
line45:
line46:         axs[k, z].plot(t, f(t), ls=":",
line47:                 color='green', marker='o', linewidth=.5, markersize=.5)
line48: axs[0, 0].plot(t, fourier_coeffs(f, 2)[0], label='n=2', ls=":",
```

Chapter 6

```
line49:                  color='red', marker='o', linewidth=.25, markersize=.5)
line50: axs[0, 1].plot(t, fourier_coeffs(f, 5)[0], label='n=5', ls=":",
line51:                  color='red', marker='o', linewidth=.25, markersize=.5)
line52: axs[1, 0].plot(t, fourier_coeffs(f, 10)[0], label='n=10', ls=":",
line53:                  color='red', marker='o', linewidth=.25, markersize=.5)
line54: axs[1, 1].plot(t, fourier_coeffs(f, 15)[0], label='n=15', ls=":",
line55:                  color='red', marker='o', linewidth=.25, markersize=.5)
line56: fig.suptitle('periodic square-wave waveform')
line57: fig.legend()
line58: for ax in axs.flat:
line59:     ax.set(xlabel='t', ylabel='Amplitude')
line60:
line61: for ax in axs.flat:
line62:     ax.label_outer()
line63: plt.show()
```

Chapter 6

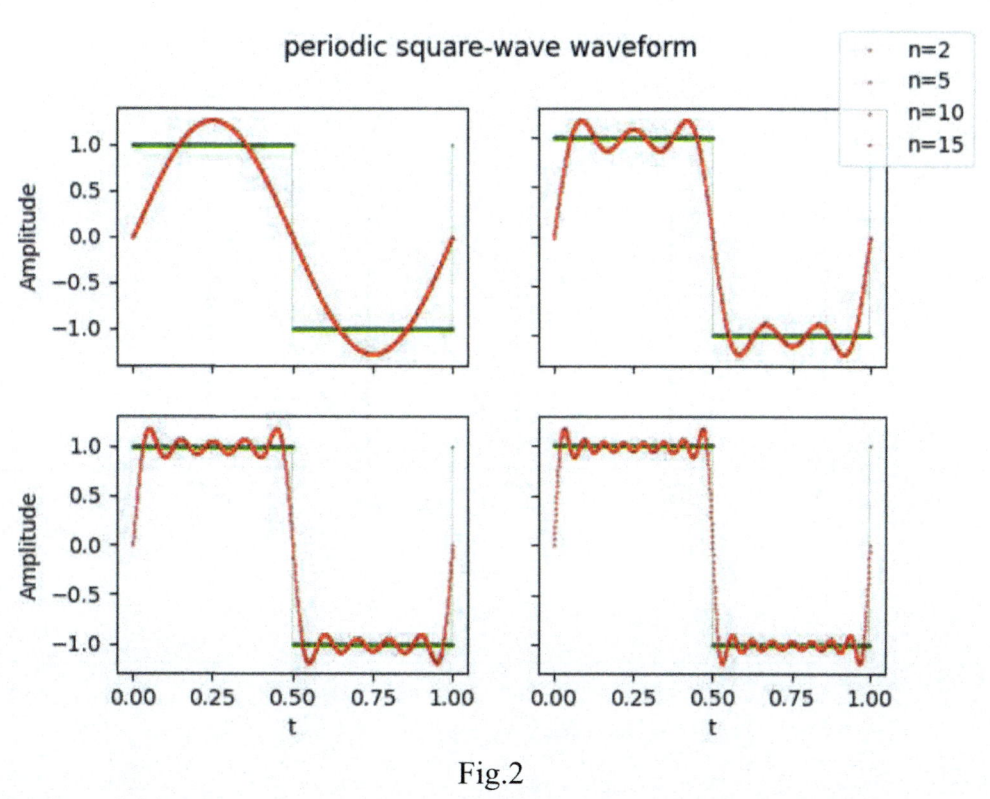

Fig.2

Saw tooth

This program can easily demonstrate and calculate the valued of Fourier series for any kind of periodic function.

For example, in the below, instead of using square wave, saw tooth wave is defined and calculations are returned based on this function.

The general shape of saw tooth wave is like figure3.

Chapter 6

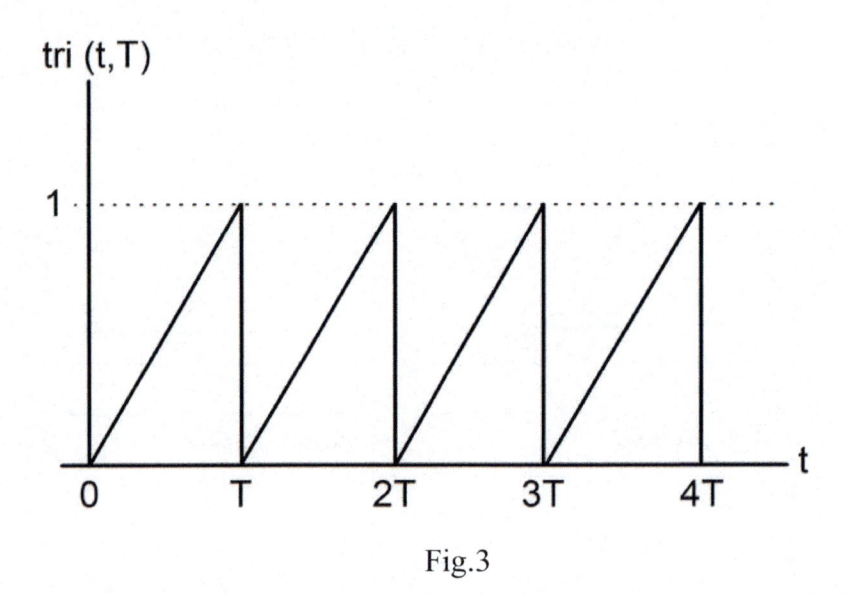

tri (t,T)

Fig.3

```
line1 :import numpy as np
line2 :import math
line3 :from scipy.signal import square
line4 :from scipy.signal import sawtooth
line5 :import matplotlib.pyplot as plt
line6 :import scipy.integrate as spi
line7 :'''
line8 :time management period
line9 :'''
line10:t = np.linspace(0, 1, 1000, endpoint=True)
line11:'''
line12:periodic function
line13:'''
line14:p = 1
line15:
line16:def f(t):
line17:    return sawtooth(5*np.pi*t)
line18:
line19:'''
line20:an , bn
line21:'''
line22:
line23:def fourier_coeffs(func, i):
line24:    a_coeff = []
line25:    b_coeff = []
line26:    for n in range(i+1):
line27:        an = (2./p) * spi.quad(lambda t: func(t) *
line28:                        np.cos(2 * np.pi * n * t / p), 0, p)[0]
line29:        bn = (2./p) * spi.quad(lambda t: func(t) *
line30:                        np.sin(2 * np.pi * n * t / p), 0, p)[0]
line31:        a_coeff.append(an)
```

Chapter 6

```
line32:            b_coeff.append(bn)
line33:        formula = 0.5*np.array(a_coeff)[0]
line34:    for n in range(0, len(a_coeff)):
line35:        formula = formula + \
line36:            +np.array(a_coeff)[n] * np.cos(2. * np.pi * n * t / p) + \
line37:            np.array(b_coeff)[n] * np.sin(2. * np.pi * n * t / p)
line38:
line39:    return formula, a_coeff, b_coeff
line40:
line41:i = [0, 1]
line42:j = [0, 1]
line43:fig, axs = plt.subplots(2, 2)
line44:for k in i:
line45:    for z in j:
line46:
line47:        axs[k, z].plot(t, f(t),  ls=":",
line48:                        color='green', marker='o', linewidth=.5, markersize=.5)
line49:axs[0, 0].plot(t, fourier_coeffs(f, 2)[0], label='n=2', ls=":",
line50:                color='red', marker='o', linewidth=.25, markersize=.5)
line51:axs[0, 1].plot(t, fourier_coeffs(f, 5)[0], label='n=5', ls=":",
line52:                color='red', marker='o', linewidth=.25, markersize=.5)
line53:axs[1, 0].plot(t, fourier_coeffs(f, 10)[0], label='n=10', ls=":",
line54:                color='red', marker='o', linewidth=.25, markersize=.5)
line55:axs[1, 1].plot(t, fourier_coeffs(f, 15)[0], label='n=15', ls=":",
line56:                color='red', marker='o', linewidth=.25, markersize=.5)
line57:fig.suptitle('periodic square-wave waveform')
line58:fig.legend()
line59:for ax in axs.flat:
line60:    ax.set(xlabel='t', ylabel='Amplitude')
line61:
line62:for ax in axs.flat:
line63:    ax.label_outer()
line64:plt.show()
line65:
```

Chapter 6

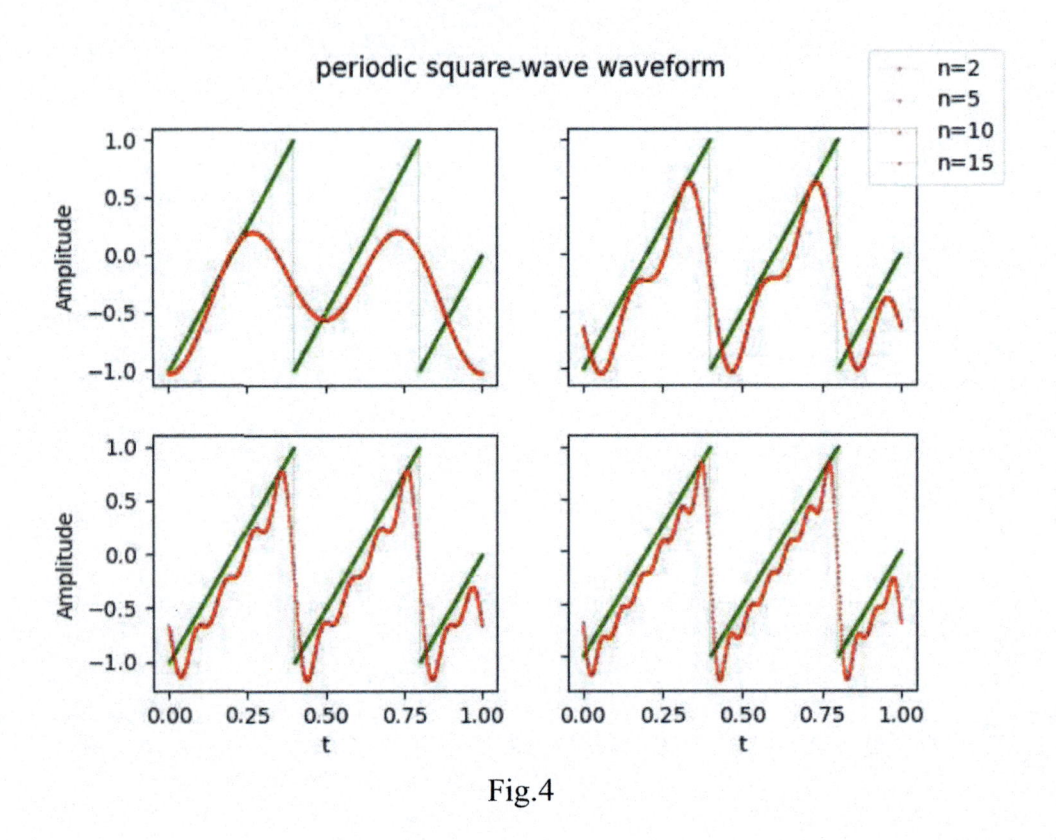

periodic square-wave waveform

Fig.4

Chapter 6

Chapter 7

Single degree of freedom system

In this project, response of a single degree freedom system with defined mass and damping ratio to harmonic loads will be discussed.

The general shape of a single degree of freedom is displayed in figure1.

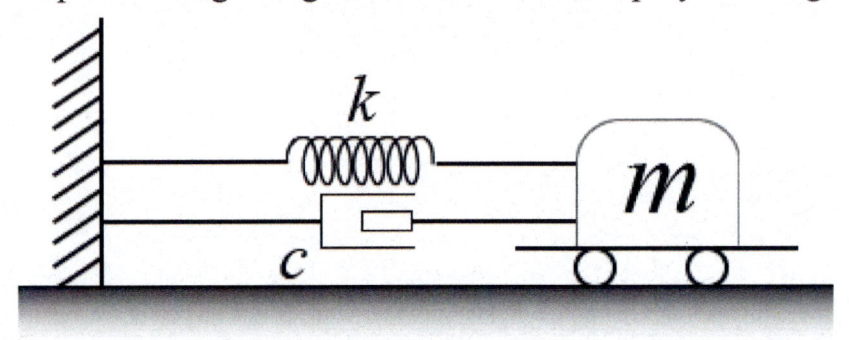

Fig.1

Dynamic parameters and response plot will be depicted.

Line1-Line3: Importing the required libraries

Line4: Redefining pi value with a simple notation

Line7: Defining the main function which has related arguments including mass, damping ratio, harmonic force value, frequency of the force, static force, static deflection, total time, time steps.

Name of the argument	Symbol in formulas	Symbol in python script
Mass	m	m
Damping ratio	ξ	xi
Harmonic force value	p	p
Frequency of the force	f	f
Static force	p_{st}	p_static
Static deflection	δ	Delta_static

Chapter 7

Total time	t	t$_{max}$
Time step		time_step

Line8: Angular frequency of harmonic force
$$\omega(\frac{rad}{\sec}) = 2\pi f$$
Line9: Stiffness
$$k(\frac{N}{m}) = \frac{p_{st}}{\delta}$$
Line10: Angular natural frequency
$$\omega_n(\frac{rad}{\sec}) = \sqrt{\frac{k}{m}}$$
Line11: Natural frequency
$$f(Hz) = \frac{\omega_n}{2\pi}$$
Line12: Period of oscillation
$$T(\sec) = \frac{1}{f}$$
Line13: Frequency ratio
$$\beta = \frac{\omega}{\omega_n}$$
Line14: Dynamic magnification factor
$$DMF = \frac{1}{\sqrt{(1-\beta^2)^2 + (2\beta\xi)^2}}$$

Line15: phase shift between force and steady-state response
$$\phi = tg^{-1}(\frac{2\beta\xi}{1-\beta^2})$$
Line16-Line24:
Simple outputs so far.
Line25-Line36:

Chapter 7

$$u_{(t)} = transient + steady-state$$

$$transient = e^{-\xi\omega_n t}[A\sin(\omega_d t) + b\cos(\omega_d t)]$$

$$steady-state = \frac{p_0}{k}[\frac{1}{(1-\beta^2)^2 + (2\beta\xi)^2}][(1-\beta^2)\sin(\omega t) - 2\xi\beta\cos(\omega t)]$$

Firstly, A and B constants should be defined. To do so, initial condition should be applied in the equation. Most of the structural engineering problems like this start with no motion at the beginning. Therefore, $u_{(t=0)} = 0$ and $\dot{u}_{(t=0)} = 0$ which mean both the position and velocity are equal to zero.

To differentiate the equation, there are various methods; however, one of the most well-known methods is substitution like below. This makes the equation easier to follow.

$$\Omega = \frac{p_0}{k}[\frac{1}{(1-\beta^2) + (2\xi\beta)^2}]$$

$$c_1 = \Omega(1-\beta^2)$$

$$c_2 = -\Omega 2\xi\beta$$

Here some calculation details are not discussed and the final result is shown.
After applying initial conditions, we have:

$$A = \frac{1}{\omega_d}(c_1\omega + c_2\xi\omega_n)$$

$$B = -c_2$$

Line38-Line50:
Plots the below values over time:
Transient response
Static displacement
Steady-state amplitude
Steady-state response

Line 53-Line60:
Plots combined response which is the sum of transient response and steady-state response

$$combined\_response = e^{-\xi\omega_n t}[A\sin(\omega_d t) + b\cos(\omega_d t)] + \frac{p_0}{k}[\frac{1}{(1-\beta^2)^2 + (2\beta\xi)^2}][(1-\beta^2)\sin(\omega t) - 2\xi\beta\cos(\omega t)]$$

Chapter 7

```python
line1 : import math
line2 : import numpy as np
line3 : import matplotlib.pyplot as plt
line4 : pi = math.pi
line5 :
line6 :
line7 : def dynamic_param(m, xi, p, f, p_static, delta_static, tmax, time_step):
line8 :     omega = 2*pi*f
line9 :     k = p_static/(delta_static/1000)
line10:     omega_n = round(math.sqrt(k/m), 3)
line11:     f_n = round(omega_n/(2*math.pi), 3)
line12:     T = round(1/f_n, 2)
line13:     beta = omega/omega_n
line14:     DMF = 1/math.sqrt((1-beta**2)**2 + (2*xi*beta)**2)
line15:     phase = math.atan((2*xi*beta)/(1-beta**2))
line16:     print('The frequency ratio is {one}.'.format(one=round(beta, 3)))
line17:     print('The dynamic magnification factor is {one}.'.format(
line18:         one=round(DMF, 3)))
line19:     print(' static deflection of {one} m.\
line20:         The DMF indicates a steady-state dynamic amplitude of {two} m.'.format(
line21:         one=round(p/k, 4), two=(round(DMF*p/k, 4))))
line22:     print('The phase difference between force and response is {one} radians\
line23:             or {two} degrees.'.format(
line24:         one=round(phase, 3), two=round(phase*180/pi, 1)))
line25:     O = (p/k)*(1/((1-beta**2)**2 + (2*xi*beta)**2))
line26:     C1 = O*(1-beta**2)
line27:     C2 = -O*2*xi*beta
line28:     omega_d = omega_n*math.sqrt(1-xi**2)
line29:     A = (-1/omega_d)*(C2*xi*omega_n + C1*omega)
line30:     B = -C2
line31:
line32:     steps = tmax/time_step
line33:     t = np.linspace(0, tmax, int(steps))
line34:
line35:     ut = math.e**(-xi*omega_n*t)*(A*np.sin(omega_d*t) + B*np.cos(omega_d*t))
line36:     us = O*((1-beta**2)*np.sin(omega*t) - 2*xi*beta*np.cos(omega*t))
line37:
line38:     fig, ax = plt.subplots()
line39:
line40:     ax.plot(t, ut, '-', label='Transient response')
line41:     ax.plot([0, tmax], [p/k, p/k], 'g', label='Static displacement')
line42:     ax.plot([0, tmax], [DMF*p/k, DMF*p/k], 'r', label='Steady-state amplitude')
line43:     ax.plot(t, us, '-', label='Steady-state response')
line44:     ax.set_xlim([0, tmax])
line45:     ax.set_xlabel('Time (sec)')
line46:     ax.set_ylabel('Displacement (m)')
line47:     ax.set_title('displacement-time history')
line48:     ax.grid()
line49:     ax.legend(loc='lower right')
line50:     plt.show()
line51:
line52:     fig, ax = plt.subplots()
line53:     ax.plot(t, (ut+us), label='Combined response')
```

```
line54:     ax.set_xlim([0, tmax])
line55:     ax.set_xlabel('Time (sec)')
line56:     ax.set_ylabel('Displacement (m)')
line57:     ax.set_title('ut+us displacement-time history')
line58:     ax.grid()
line59:     ax.legend(loc='lower right')
line60:     plt.show()
line61:     return
```

Example1:

Let's say the constants are due to the table:

Constants	Value	Unit
m	10000	kg
ξ	0.05	---
p	600	N
f	0.9	Hz
p_static	1500	N
delta_static	7	mm

Out

The frequency ratio is 1.222.

The dynamic magnification factor is 1.971.

Static deflection of 0.0028 m. The DMF indicates a steady-state dynamic amplitude of 0.0055 m.

The phase difference between force and response is -0.243 radians or -13.9 degrees.

Chapter 7

displacement-time history

ut+us displacement-time history

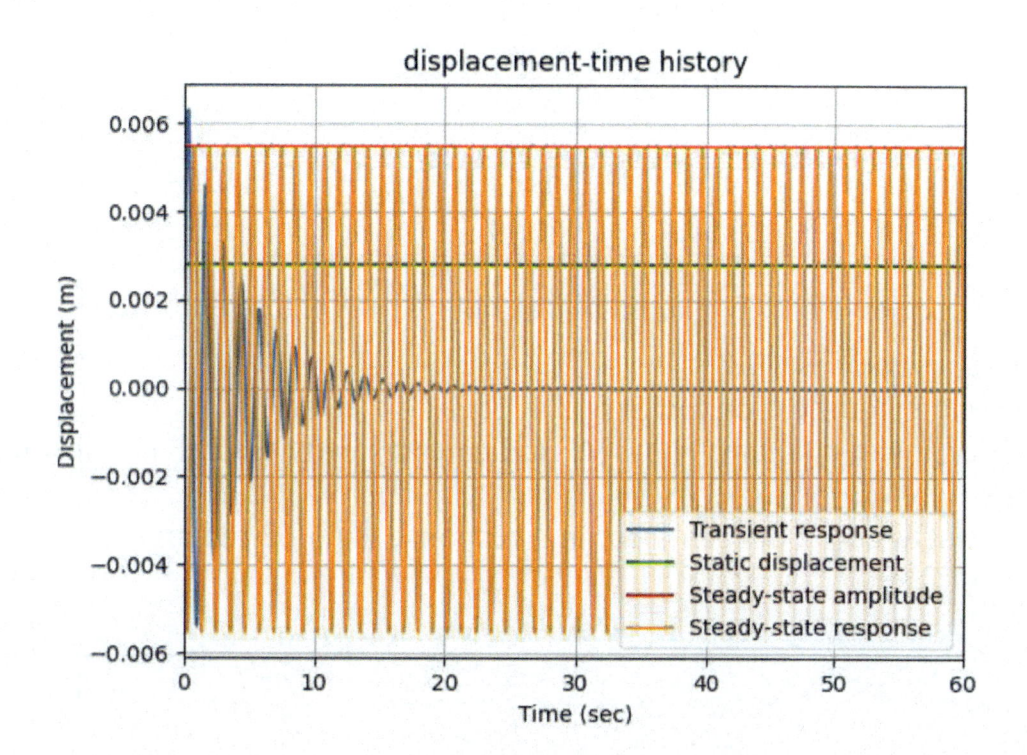

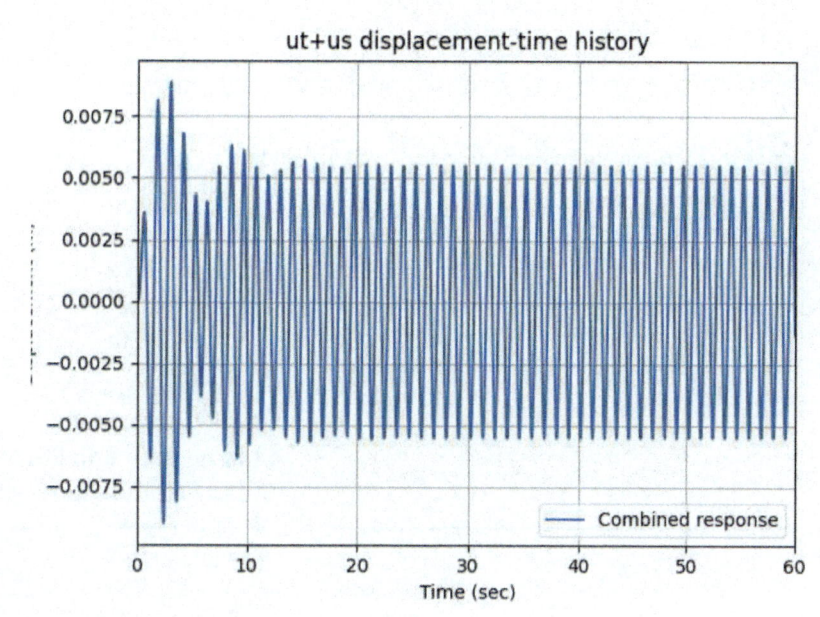

Example2:
Let's say the constants are due to the table:

116

Chapter 7

constants	value	unit
m	5000	kg
ξ	0.02	---
p	600	N
f	0.9	Hz
p_static	3000	N
delta_static	10	mm

The frequency ratio is 0.73.
The dynamic magnification factor is 2.137.
Static deflection of 0.002 m. The DMF indicates a steady-state dynamic amplitude of 0.0043 m.
The phase difference between force and response is 0.062 radians or 3.6 degrees.

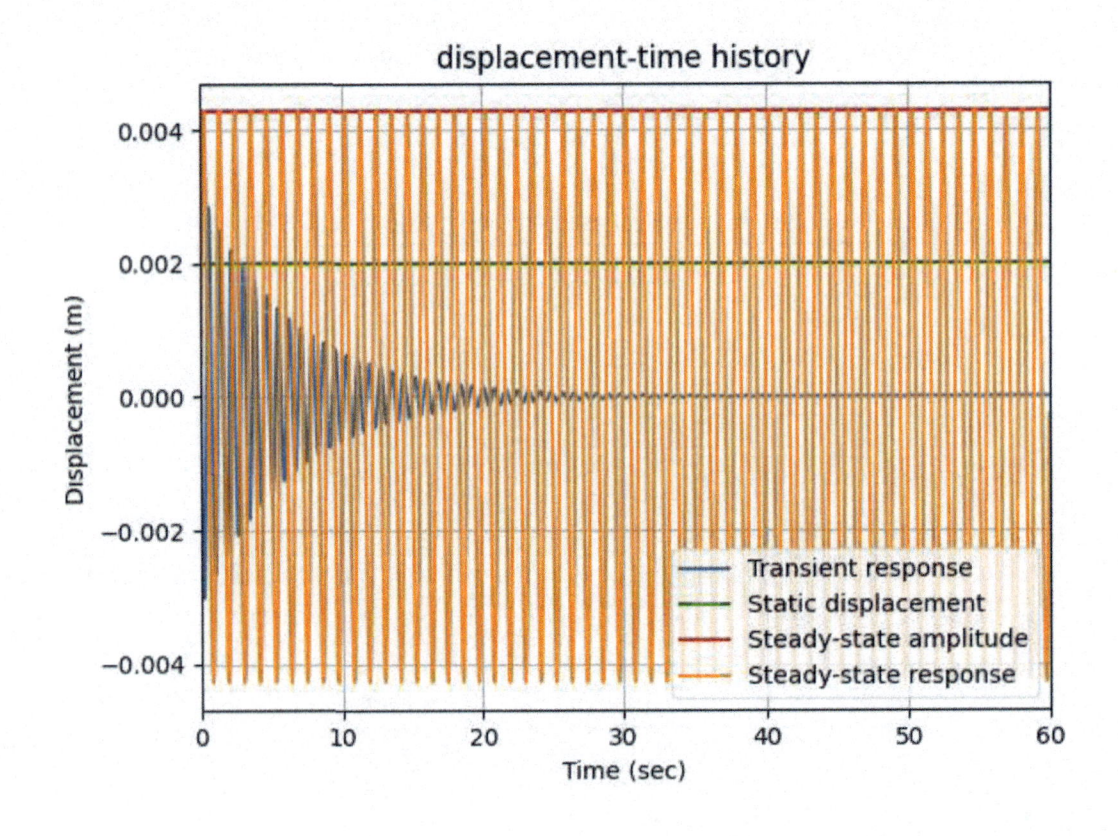

117

Chapter 7

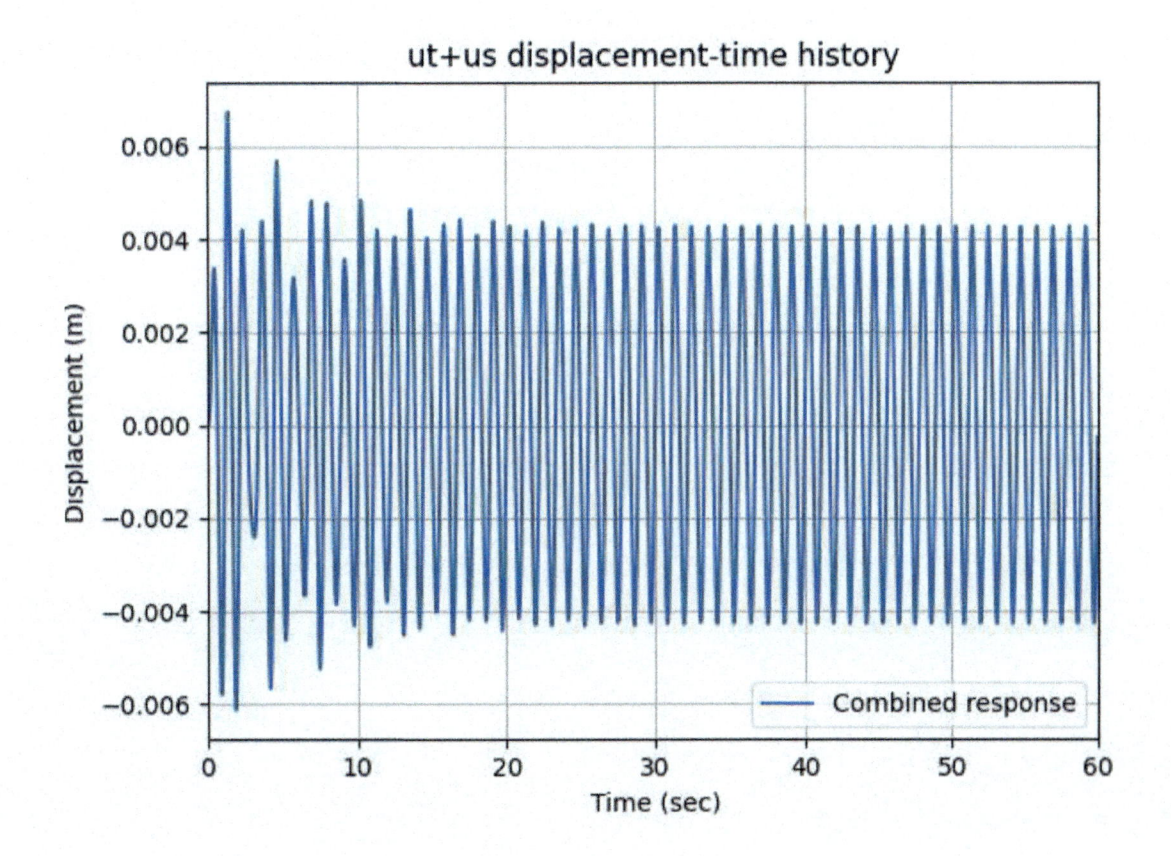

ut+us displacement-time history

Chapter 7

Chapter 8

Chapter 8

Concrete bean design

Analysis and design of reinforced concrete sections subjected to flexural moments is always a crucial area of study. Many of the structural elements such as beams are frequently exposed to flexure throughout their lifespan. The causes of this moment could vary from case to case however; common sources include dead, live, snow, earthquake, and wind loads. Here Loads are not the main subject and the focus is actually on the reinforced concrete itself.

For further evaluation a $p-\delta$ graph under pure bending is depicted as figure1. Different parts of this graph could be categorized as:

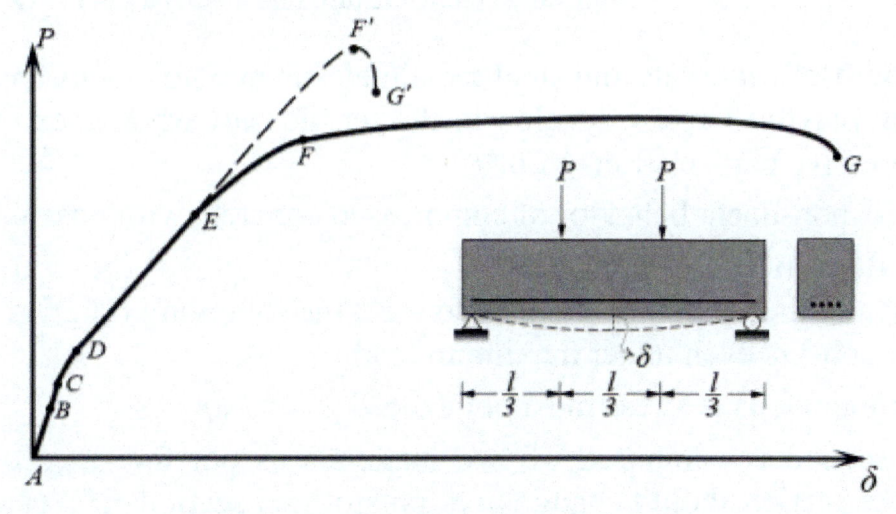

Fig.1- $p-\delta$ graph under pure bending

AB: linear behavior without cracks
BC: Emergence of Plastic deflections in the tensile part
C: cracking

120

Chapter 8

CD: increase in the number of cracks
DE: Opening of cracks and linear behavior of compressive part of the section
EF: Non-linear behavior of concrete and elastic behavior of longitudinal bars
F: Yield of tension reinforcement
FG: increase of non-linear behavior of concrete
G: Failure

Behavior of a section toward flexure, based on the affecting moment, could be described as follows:

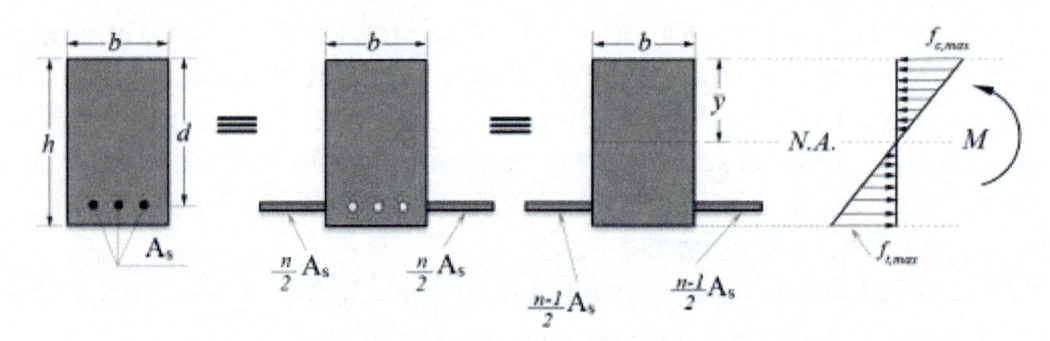

Fig.2- section subjected to flexure (elastic behavior)

1. **Elastic:** Both concrete and steel remain elastic and no cracks appear
2. **Elasto-plastic:** Cracks develop in the tensile part while maximum stress in compressive parts restricts to $0.5f'_c$
3. **Plastic:** non-linear behavior of compressed concrete with possibility of failure

Elastic design

The design of the section is intended to meet the following criteria:
No crack appears even under maximum load

The maximum tensile stress must not exceed $f_r = 0.7\sqrt{f'_c}$

Since a section is composed of two materials as per the rules of strength of materials, the section should change to a transformed section. The calculations and formulas are as below:

Chapter 8

Table1- definition of signs in equations

Sign	Definition
$\bar{y}$	Distance between farthest compressive fiber from neutral axis
$f_{t,max}$	Stress of the farthest tensile fiber
$f_{c,max}$	Stress of the farthest compressive fiber
M_{cr}	Cracking moment
I_{tr}	Transformed moment of inertia

In the first place, neutral axis and transformed moment of inertia should be calculated:

$$\bar{y} = \frac{\sum Ay}{\sum A} = \frac{0.5bh^2 + (n-1)A_s d}{bh + (n-1)A_s} \qquad \text{Equation 1}$$

$$I_{tr} = \sum(I_0 + AD^2) = \frac{1}{12}bh^3 + bh(\frac{h}{2} - \bar{y})^2 + (n-1)A_s(d - \bar{y})^2 \qquad \text{Equation 2}$$

The stress values for concrete and critical fibers are calculated as follows:

$$f_{t,max} = \frac{M(h - \bar{y})}{I_{tr}} \leq f_r \qquad \text{Equation 3}$$

$$f_{c,max} = \frac{M\bar{y}}{I_{tr}} \qquad \text{Equation 4}$$

$$f_s = n\frac{M(d - \bar{y})}{I_{tr}} \qquad \text{Equation 5}$$

$$M_{cr} = \frac{f_r I_{tr}}{h - \bar{y}} \qquad \text{Equation 6}$$

Chapter 8

Elasto-plastic design

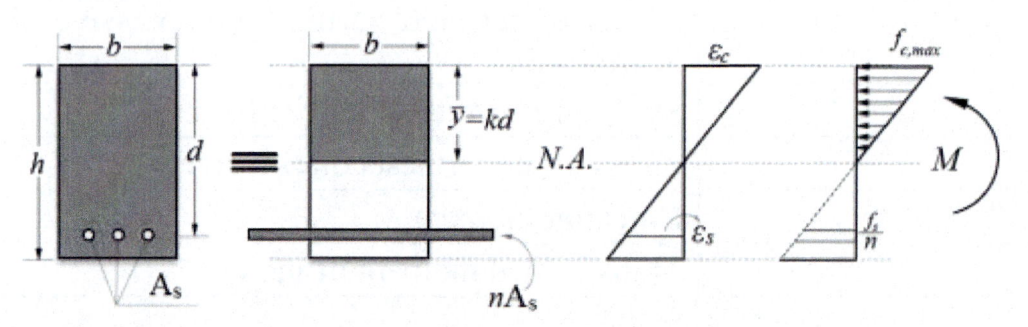

Fig.3- section subjected to flexure (elasto-plastic behavior)

Concrete in compressive part remains linear ($f_{c,\max} < 0.5 f_c'$) although it is cracked in tensile part. In an elasto-plastic scenario, concrete has a significantly lower tension capacity below the neutral axis. However, due to safety and simplicity this limited capacity is not factored into calculations.

Table2- definition of signs in equations

Sign	Definition
$\bar{y}$	Distance between farthest compressive fiber from neutral axis
$f_{t,\max}$	Stress of the farthest tensile fiber
$f_{c,\max}$	Stress of the farthest compressive fiber
M_{cr}	Maximum tolerable moment
I_{tr}	Transformed moment of inertia

$$\bar{y} = \frac{\sum Ay}{\sum A} = \frac{(b\bar{y})(\bar{y}/2) + nA_s d}{b\bar{y} + nA_s} \quad \text{Equation 6}$$

$$\bar{y}^2 + \frac{2nA_s}{b}\bar{y} - \frac{2nA_s d}{b} = 0 \quad \text{Equation 7}$$

Chapter 8

$$\bar{y} = kd \quad \text{Equation 8}$$

$$\rho = \frac{A_s}{bd} \quad \text{Equation 9}$$

$$k^2 + 2n\rho k - 2n\rho = 0$$
$$k = -n\rho + \sqrt{n^2\rho^2 + 2n\rho} \quad \text{Equation 10}$$

$$I_{tr} = \sum(I_0 + AD^2) = \frac{1}{3}b\bar{y}^3 + nA_s(d-\bar{y})^2 \quad \text{Equation 11}$$

Stress value for both concrete and bars could be calculated using aforementioned equations.

Line1-Line4: required libraries are imported.

Line5-Line8: default values for mechanical properties of concrete and steel bars.

Line11-Line21: the function responsible for elastic analysis of the section by equations1-equations6. The function returns.

1. Stress of the farthest compressive fiber
2. Cracking moment
3. Stress of the farthest tensile fiber

NB: Line12: `abar` is the total area of bars

Line24-line63: the function responsible for elasto-plastic analysis of the section by equations1-equations6. The function returns eventually returns the maximum tolerable moment for the section.

NB: Line24-Line25: defines the main function with basic geometrical properties. In addition, the availability of compression bars is set to False by default; having said that, if they exist c_bars must be True and respective values for bars should be defined in c_phi for the bars diameter and c_numphi for the number of bars.

NB: Line26-Line36: if the compression bars do not exist, governing equations should be equation6 to equation11.

NB: Line37-Line55: if the compression bars exist, governing equations should change to the following equations:

$$\bar{y} = \frac{\sum Ay}{\sum A} = \frac{(b\bar{y})(\bar{y}/2) + nA_s d + (2n-1)A'_s d'}{b\bar{y} + nA_s + nA_s + (2n-1)A'_s} \quad \text{Equation 12}$$

124

Chapter 8

$$\bar{y} = k'd$$
$$\rho = \frac{A'_s}{bd}$$
Equation 13

$$k' = -[n\rho + (2n-1)\rho'] + \sqrt{(n\rho + (2n-1)\rho')^2 + 2n\rho + 2(2n-1)\rho'(\frac{d}{d'})}$$
Equation 14

NB: Line53-Line54: then calculated M_{cr} should be compared with allowable stress show in table3. If M_{cr} meets the criteria, it is acceptable.

Table3- allowable stress according to AIC

Allowable stress in concrete	Allowable stress for steel	
$0.45f'_c$	G280, G350	G420
	140	170

NB: Line55-Line63: If M_{cr} does not meet the criteria, then the reference point for calculating M_{cr}, will change to maximum allowable stress for steel.

```
line1 :import math
line2 :import pandas as pd
line3 :import numpy as np
line4 :import matplotlib.pyplot as plt
line5 :fy = 400
line6 :fc = 30
line7 :es = 200000
line8 :fmax_steel = 170
line9 :
line10:
line11:def elastic_approach(b, h, d, phi, numphi):
line12:    abar = numphi*(np.pi)*.25*(phi**2)
line13:    fr = 0.7*np.sqrt(fc)
line14:    ec = 4700*np.sqrt(fc)
line15:    n = es/ec
line16:    ybar = (b*0.5*h**2+(n-1)*abar*d)/(b*h+(n-1)*abar)
line17:    Itr = (b*h**3)/12+b*h*(0.5*h-ybar)**2+(n-1)*abar*(d-ybar)**2
line18:    Mcr = fr*Itr/(h-ybar)
line19:    fcmax = Mcr*ybar/Itr
line20:    fs = n*Mcr*(d-ybar)/Itr
line21:    return fcmax, Mcr, fs
line22:
line23:
line24:def elasto_plastic_approach(b, h, d, phi, numphi, c_bars=False,
```

```python
line25:                         c_phi=False, c_numphi=False):
line26:     if c_bars == False:
line27:         abar = numphi*math.pi*.25*phi**2
line28:         fr = 0.7*math.sqrt(fc)
line29:         ec = 4700*math.sqrt(fc)
line30:         n = es/ec
line31:         rho = abar/(b*d)
line32:         k = np.sqrt(2*n*rho+(n*rho)**2)-(n*rho)
line33:         j = 1-k/3
line34:         Mcr = 0.45*fc*k*j*b*(d**2)/2
line35:         fs = Mcr/(abar*j*d)
line36:         return fs, Mcr, n, k, abar, j
line37:     elif c_bars == True:
line38:         abar = numphi*math.pi*.25*phi**2
line39:         cabar = c_numphi*math.pi*.25*c_phi**2
line40:         fr = 0.7*math.sqrt(fc)
line41:         ec = 4700*math.sqrt(fc)
line42:         n = es/ec
line43:         rho = abar/(b*d)
line44:         crho = cabar/(b*d)
line45:         k = math.sqrt(2*n*rho+(n*rho)**2)-(n*rho)
line46:         ck = -(n*rho+(n*2-1)*crho)+math.sqrt((n*rho+(2*n-1)*crho)
line47:                     ** 2+2*n*rho
line48:                     +2*(2*n-1)*crho*((h-d)/d))
line49:         ybar = ck*d
line50:         j = 1-k/3
line51:         Itr = ((0.33*b*ybar**3)+(2*n-1)*cabar*(ybar-(h-d))**2+
line52:             n*abar*(d-ybar)**2)
line53:         Mcr = 0.45*fc*Itr/ybar
line54:         fs = n*Mcr*(d-ybar)/Itr
line55:         if fs < fmax_steel:
line56:             return ybar, ck, Itr, Mcr
line57:         elif fs > fmax_steel:
line58:             print('''stress of bars exceeded the maximum allowable stress,\
line59:                 therefore,\n maximum moment is
line60:                     calculated based on the allowable stress of \
line61:                 compression reinforcement ''')
line62:             Mcr = fmax_steel*Itr/(n*(d-ybar))
line63:             return Mcr
```

Example:

Line1-Line5: imports the required libraries

NB: Line5: imports the main functions from python file called concrete_beam.py

Line8-Line12: defines numpy arrays of geometrical properties of section:

NB: line11-Line12: three bars have 30mm diameter in all sections

126

Chapter 8

Line14-Line30: forming a dictionary with defined values in order to create two pandas DataFrames named `df_elastic` and `df_elasto_plastic`, respectively.

Line35-Line44: makes the graph which is formed based on M_{cr} from two approaches.

```python
line1 :import numpy as np
line2 :import matplotlib.pyplot as plt
line3 :import pandas as pd
line4 :
line5 :from concrete_beam import elastic_approach, elasto_plastic_approach
line6 :
line7 :
line8 :b = np.arange(250, 500, 20)
line9 :h = np.ones(len(b))*500
line10:d = h-50
line11:phi = np.ones(len(b))*30
line12:numphi = np.ones(len(b))*3
line13:
line14:dimensions_dict = {'b': b, 'h': h,
line15:                   'd': d, 'phi': phi, 'numphi': numphi}
line16:
line17:df_elastic = pd.DataFrame(data=dimensions_dict)
line18:
line19:df_elasto_plastic = pd.DataFrame(data=dimensions_dict)
line20:df_elastic['cracking_moment(N.mm)'] = (elastic_approach(df_elastic['b'],
line21:                                      df_elastic['h'],
line22:                                      df_elastic['d'],
line23:                                      df_elastic['phi'],
line24:                                      df_elastic['numphi'])[1]/1e6)
line25:df_elasto_plastic['cracking_moment(N.mm)'] = (
line26:    elasto_plastic_approach(df_elasto_plastic['b'],
line27:                            df_elasto_plastic['h'],
line28:                            df_elasto_plastic['d'],
line29:                            df_elasto_plastic['phi'],
line30:                            df_elasto_plastic['numphi'])[1]/1e6)
line31:
line32:
line33:
line34:
line35:fig, ax = plt.subplots()
line36:ax.bar(df_elastic['b'], df_elastic['cracking_moment(N.mm)'],
line37:       color='b', width=5)
line38:ax.bar(df_elasto_plastic['b']+5,
line39:       df_elasto_plastic['cracking_moment(N.mm)'], color='r', width=5)
line40:ax.set_xlabel('b(mm)')
line41:ax.set_ylabel('cracking moment(N.mm)')
line42:fig.legend(['elastic analysis', 'elasto plastic analysis'])
line43:fig.suptitle('b versus cracking moment')
line44:plt.show()
```

Chapter 8

As shown in Figure 4, elsto_plastic approach with acceptance of cracks could lead to more than 100% values in M_{cr} in comparison with elastic_approach which is obviously a conservative approach.

For example, with $b = 250mm$, the M_{cr} value stands at $125 kN.m$ while the very same value for elasto_plastic approach is $50 kN.m$.

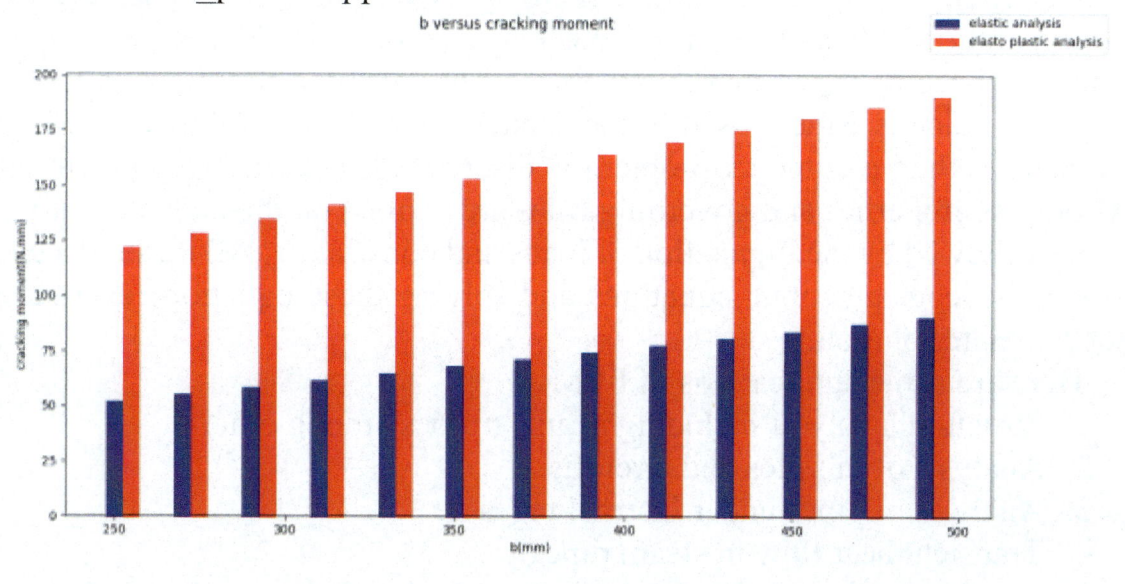

Fig.4-cracking moment for sections with elastic and elasto-plastic behavior

128

Chapter 9

Chapter9

Finite element method for beams

It is often very difficult and challenging as well as time-consuming to find the exact solutions for solid or fluid mechanics problems. That is why approximate solutions become much more convenient. One of these Solutions is finite element method, which is widely used in mechanical and a structural analysis. In the finite element method a complex problem is discretized into simple geometrical shapes. After this, properties and governing rules are applied on the elements and elemental nodes followed by the imposition of loads and constraints. All these procedures lead to simultaneous algebraic equations and solving these equations eventuates in the approximate solution.

Here are some applications of FEM:
1. Structural analysis including beams trusses among others
2. Analysis of missiles and aircrafts
3. Analysis of pipes under internal pressure
4. Transient heat flow in steam pipes

In this chapter though FEM equations and relationships will only be represented for beams. For the sake of simplicity, the code contains the following features:
1. Only concentrated loads are defined
2. Nodes and other features along with the basic parameters such as material properties, length of elements and status of nodes in accordance with degree of freedom should be defined by the user
3. The code supports the existence of non-prismatic elements

Unlike previous chapters, every milestone in the code is discussed separately in order to make the code easier to follow:

NB: all codes in this part are for example1.

Example1

Find the reactions and displacements of node number 1,2 and 3.

Chapter 9

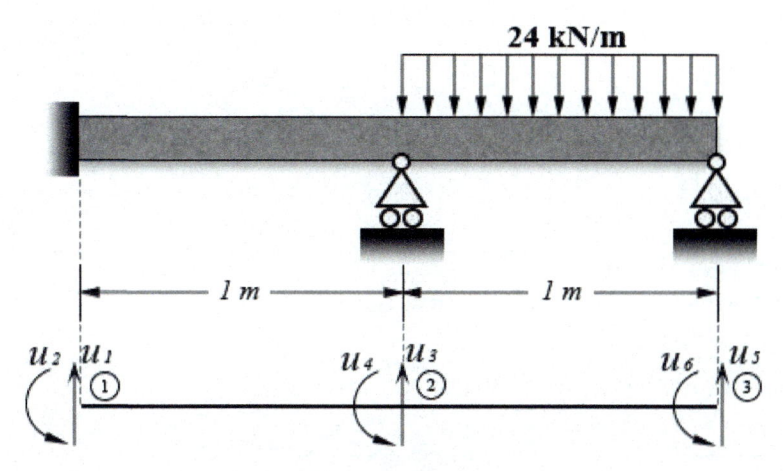

Fig.1-Example1

A) Required libraries and inputs:
Libraries: numpy and matplotlib.pyplot

Table1-inputs of the code

Python variable	Explanation	Data type
Nodes	Location of nodes	list
Elastic_module	Module of elasticity for each element	Numpy array
Inertia	Moment of inertia for each element	Numpy array
l	Length of each element	Numpy array
lst	List containing local stiffness matrices	List
Lst_distributed	List containing amount of distributed loads for every element	List
u	Degrees of freedom status for every node	List
u_array	u in numpy array	Numpy array
Force	Concentrated load for every node	List
Force_array	f in numpy array	Numpy array

130

Chapter 9

Code for example1:

```
line1 :import numpy as np
line2 :import matplotlib.pyplot as plt
line3 :nodes = [0, 1, 2]
line4 :elastic_module = np.array([200e9, 200e9], dtype=np.float64)
line5 :b = np.array([0, -24000])
line6 :inertia = np.array([5e-6, 5e-6], dtype=np.float64)
line7 :l = np.array([1, 1], dtype=np.float64)
line8 :lst = []
line9 :lst_distributed = []
line10:
line11:u = [0, 0, 0, 'False', 0, 'False']
line12:force = ['False', 'False', 'False', -2000, 'False', 2000]
line13:force_array = np.array(force)
line14:u_array = np.asarray(u)
```

B) Forming the stiffness matrix:

The main formula for the stiffness matrix is equation1. Nevertheless, this matrix is formed for every element and finally all the matrices are assembled into a unit matrix.

$$k_e = \frac{EI}{l^3} \begin{Bmatrix} 12 & 6l & -12 & 6l \\ 6l & 4l^2 & -6l & 2l^2 \\ -12 & -6l & 12 & -6l \\ 6l & 2l^2 & -6l & 4l^2 \end{Bmatrix} \qquad \text{Equation1}$$

Chapter 9

The code for B is:

```
line1 :# forming Ke matrix in the general way
line2 :for i, j, z in zip(elastic_module, inertia, l):
line3 :    k = (i*j/z**3)*np.matrix([[12, 6*z, -12, 6*z],
line4 :                              [6*z, 4*z**2, -6*z, 2*z**2],
line5 :                              [-12, -6*z, +12, -6*z],
line6 :                              [6*z, 2*z**2, -6*z, 4*z**2]])
line7 :    lst.append(k)
line8 :ke = np.zeros((2*len(nodes), 2*len(nodes)))
line9 :k_indexer_i = np.arange(0, len(u), 2)
line10:k_indexer_j = k_indexer_i+4
line11:for i, j, z in zip(k_indexer_i, k_indexer_j, lst):
line12:
line13:    ke[0+i:0+j, 0+i:0+j] += z
```

Line2: This loop with the help of zip method put all the values in the zip arguments one by one into equation1 which is written in line3

Line7: After creating local stiffness matrices, all matrices are positioned in 1st list.

Line8: A matrix of zeros is created to represent the empty global matrix. Size of this matrix is twice the number of nodes as every node has vertical and rotational freedom.

Line9-Line13: All values from the local matrices are placed into the global matrix using the following pattern:

$$k_e = \begin{Bmatrix} k_{11} & k_{12} & k_{13} & k_{14} & 0 & 0 \\ k_{21} & k_{22} & k_{23} & k_{24} & 0 & 0 \\ k_{31} & k_{32} & k_{33}+k'_{11} & k_{34}k'_{12} & k'_{13} & k'_{14} \\ k_{41} & k_{42} & k_{43}+k'_{21} & k_{44}+k'_{22} & k'_{23} & k'_{24} \\ 0 & 0 & k'_{31} & k'_{32} & k'_{33} & k'_{34} \\ 0 & 0 & k'_{41} & k'_{42} & k'_{43} & k'_{44} \end{Bmatrix}$$

Chapter 9

C) Forming distributed load matrix

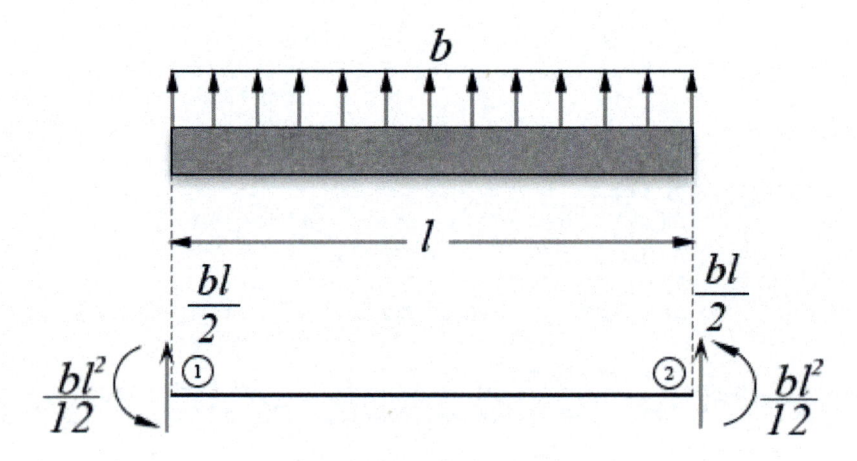

Fig.2- distributed load

$$\begin{Bmatrix} \dfrac{-bl}{2} \\ \dfrac{-bl^2}{12} \\ \dfrac{-bl}{2} \\ \dfrac{bl^2}{12} \end{Bmatrix} \qquad \text{Equation2}$$

Code:

```
line1:# forming distributed load matrix
line2:for i, j in zip(l, b):
line3:    b = np.matrix([[-i*j*.5, -j*i*i/12, -i*j*.5, j*i*i/12]])
line4:    lst_distributed.append(b)
line5:print(lst_distributed)
```

Line2-Line4: as like as local stiffness matrices, the effects of distributed loads are put to a list called `lst_distributed`

Chapter 9

D) Solving bases on defined deformations:
Code:
```
line1:index_force = np.where(force_array == 'False')
line2:ke_r = np.delete(ke, index_force[0], axis=0)
line3:ke_to_solve = np.delete(ke_r, index_force[0], axis=1)
line4:force_to_solve = np.delete(force_array, index_force[0]).astype(float)
line5:u_to_solve = np.linalg.solve(ke_to_solve, force_to_solve)
line6:index_u = np.where(u_array == 'False')
line7:np.put(u_array, index_u[0], u_to_solve)
line8:print(u_array.astype(float))
```

Line1: `index_force` is a NumPy array that contains the indices of values with a `'False'` value.

Line2-Line3: the corresponding rows and columns of `ke` derived from line1 are deleted.

Line4: also arrays with 'False' value are eliminated from `force_arrey` and saved in the `force_to_solve` NumPy array.

NB: values in the array should be float.

Line5: solves the equations of with linear algebra and puts the results in `u_to_solve`.

Line6-Line7: changes 'False' values with the calculated values in the previous line.

E) Calculating reactions:
Code:

134

Chapter 9

```
line1:# calculating reactions matrix
line2:reactions_list = []
line3:for i, j, z, k in zip(k_indexer_i, k_indexer_j, lst,
line4:                       lst_distributed):
line5:    reactions = np.matmul(z, (u_array[0+i:0+j].astype(float))
line6:                          .transpose())+k
line7:    reactions_list.append(reactions)
```

Line2: creates an empty list for putting reactions into

Line3-Line6: Based on Equation 3, the reactions are calculated and subsequently stored in the `reaction_list`.

$$\begin{Bmatrix} R_1 \\ R_2 \\ R_3 \\ R_4 \end{Bmatrix} = \frac{EI}{l^3} \begin{bmatrix} 12 & 6l & -12 & 6l \\ 6l & 4l^2 & -6l & 2l^2 \\ -12 & -6l & 12 & -6l \\ 6l & 2l^2 & -6l & 4l^2 \end{bmatrix} + \begin{Bmatrix} \dfrac{-bl}{2} \\ \dfrac{-bl^2}{12} \\ \dfrac{-bl}{2} \\ \dfrac{bl^2}{12} \end{Bmatrix} \qquad \text{Equation3}$$

F) Displaying moment diagram:
   Code:

135

Chapter 9

```
line1 :x = np.linspace(0, 2, 100)
line2 :moment_final = []
line3 :for i in x:
line4 :
line5 :    if i < 1:
line6 :        moment = np.array(reactions_list)[
line7 :            0][0][0]*i-np.array(reactions_list)[0][0][1]
line8 :        moment_final.append(moment)
line9 :    elif 1 <= i <= 2:
line10:        moment = (np.array(reactions_list)[0][0][0]*i
line11:                  -np.array(reactions_list)[0][0][1]+
line12:                  (np.array(reactions_list)[1][0][0]+2571)
line13:                  *(i-1)-24000*.5*(i-1)**2)
line14:        moment_final.append(moment)
line15:
line16:fig, ax = plt.subplots()
line17:ax.plot(x, moment_final,linestyle='--')
line18:ax.plot(x, np.zeros(len(x)),linestyle='-.')
line19:fig.suptitle('Moment diagram')
line20:ax.set_ylabel('Moment(N.m)')
line21:ax.set_xlabel('Length(m)')
line22:ax.grid()
line23:plt.show()
```

Practically, moment diagrams are drawn by utilizing previously obtained reactions

Line1: defines x which is the length of the beam.
Line2: provides and empty list for collecting moment values.
Line3-Line14: Based on the given x value, forces are considered, and the moment is calculated following the principles of statics.
Line15: moments are appended to the list created in line 2
Line16-Line23: simple graph drawing which has been thoroughly discussed in chpter4.

136

Chapter 9

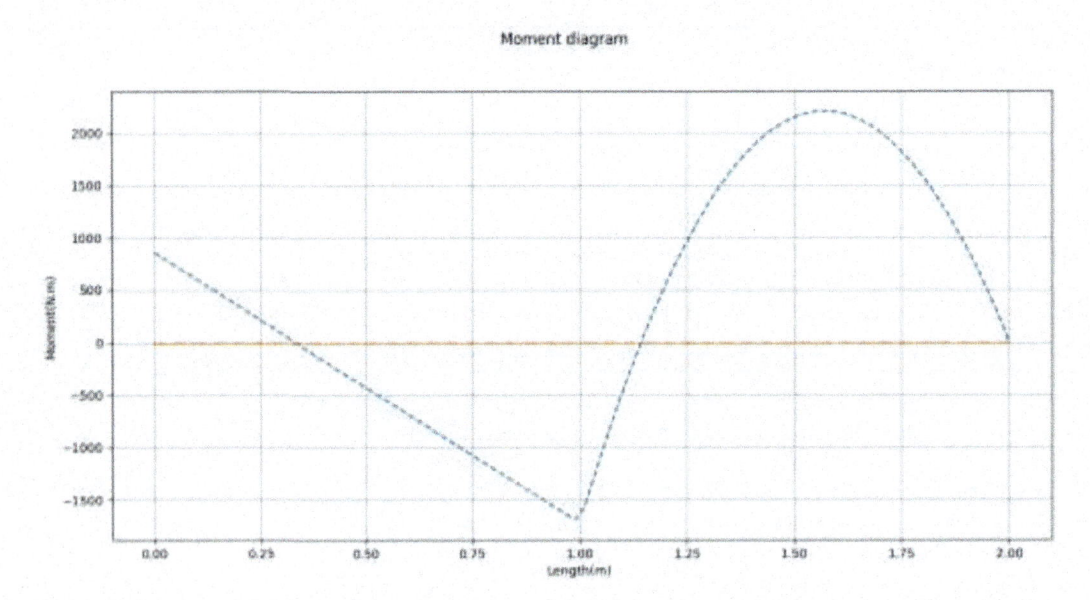

Fig.3- moment diagram of example1

Example2
Find the reactions and displacements of node number 1,2 and 3.

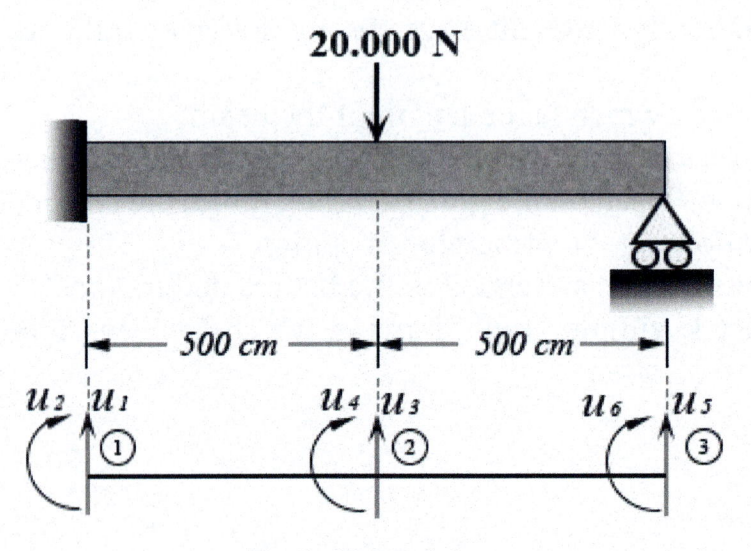

Fig.4- Example2

137

Chapter 9

```python
import numpy as np
import matplotlib.pyplot as plt
nodes = [0, 500, 1000]
elastic_module = np.array([20000000, 20000000], dtype=np.float64)
inertia = np.array([2500, 2500], dtype=np.float64)
l = np.array([500, 500], dtype=np.float64)
lst = []

u = [0, 0, 'False', 'False', 0, 'False']
force = ['False', 'False', -20000, 0, 'False', 0]
force_array = np.array(force)
u_array = np.asarray(u)
print(u_array)
# forming Ke matrix in the general way
for i, j, z in zip(elastic_module, inertia, l):
    k = (i*j/z**3)*np.matrix([[12, 6*z, -12, 6*z],
                              [6*z, 4*z**2, -6*z, 2*z**2],
                              [-12, -6*z, +12, -6*z],
                              [6*z, 2*z**2, -6*z, 4*z**2]])
    lst.append(k)
ke = np.zeros((2*len(nodes), 2*len(nodes)))
k_indexer_i = np.arange(0, len(u), 2)
k_indexer_j = k_indexer_i+4
for i, j, z in zip(k_indexer_i, k_indexer_j, lst):

    ke[0+i:0+j, 0+i:0+j] += z

# solving based on deformations
index_force = np.where(force_array == 'False')
ke_r = np.delete(ke, index_force[0], axis=0)
ke_to_solve = np.delete(ke_r, index_force[0], axis=1)
force_to_solve = np.delete(force_array, index_force[0]).astype(float)
u_to_solve = np.linalg.solve(ke_to_solve, force_to_solve)
index_u = np.where(u_array == 'False')
np.put(u_array, index_u[0], u_to_solve)
print(u_array.astype(float))

# calculating reactions matrix
reactions_list = []
for i, j, z in zip(k_indexer_i, k_indexer_j, lst):
    reactions = np.matmul(z, (u_array[0+i:0+j].astype(float)).transpose())
    reactions_list.append(reactions)
```

Chapter 9

```python
x = np.linspace(0, 1000, 200)
moment_final = []
for i in x:

    if i < 500:
        moment = (np.array(reactions_list)[0][0][0]*i
                  - np.array(reactions_list)[0][0][1])
        moment_final.append(moment)
    elif 500 <= i <= 1000:
        moment = (np.array(reactions_list)[0][0][0]*i
                  - np.array(reactions_list)[0][0][1]-20000*(i-500))
        moment_final.append(moment)

fig, ax = plt.subplots()
ax.plot(x, moment_final, linestyle='--')
ax.plot(x, np.zeros(len(x)), linestyle='-.')
fig.suptitle('Moment diagram')
ax.set_ylabel('Moment(N.m)')
ax.set_xlabel('Length(m)')
ax.grid()
plt.show()
# print(moment_final)
```

Chapter 9

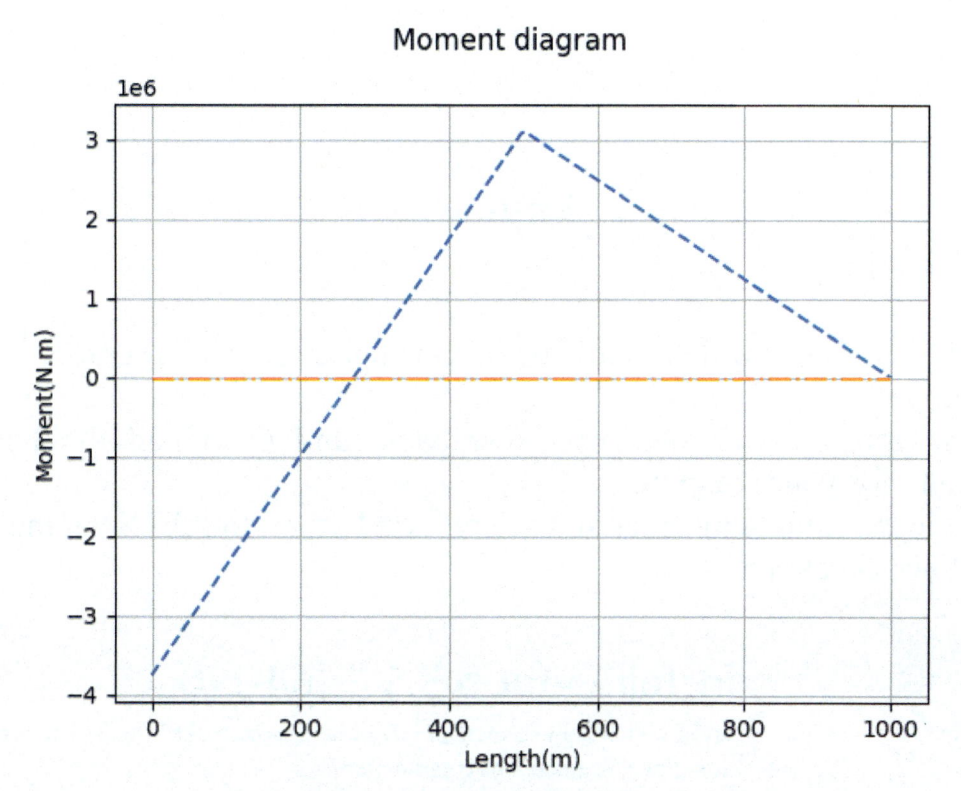

Fig.5- Diagram moment for the beam in Example2

Appendix 1

Appendix 1
Install python

There are a few steps which should be followed precisely in order to install python on your computer:
1. Go to https://www.python.org/downloads/ and download the latest stable Python3 for your computer,
2. Run the executable installer and select 'add Python to PATH' in the prompted windows checkbox

3. Verify that Python is installed,
    - Open the command prompt
    - Type Python and press enter. If Pyhton is installed, this massage pops up

Appendix 1

4. Verify that pip is installed
    - Open the command prompt
    - Type pip_v and press enter. If pip is installed, this massage pops up.

Install libraries

What is pip? Pip is a package management tool for python with which users can install the libraries they need.

To install different libraries open command prompt and write the name of the library as the following table illustrates.

Library	Syntax
Numpy	Pip install NumPy

142

Appendix 1

Pandas	`pip install pandas`
Matplotlib.pyplot	`pip install Matplotlib`
Scipy	`pip install Scipy`

Install vscode

After installing python, in order to run the code, users should also install an IDE[4] this book is written in Vscode because it offers over a wide range of extensions allowing side hand the features for having Vscode installed go to https://code.visualstudio.com/download download a version and install it.

Virtual environment

While beginners can escape this part, if you are required to install machine learning libraries such as scikit, Tensorflow and pytorch, it is highly recommended to create an isolated environment and install the necessary libraries within this environment.
1. Create a main folder. In this case we called it test.
2. Open vscode
3. Open new folder from file and select test folder
4. In explorer, Test opens
5. Crete a new file. We called it file.py
6. After creating the file, right click on it and selec open in integrated Terminal

---

[4] integrated development environment

Appendix 1

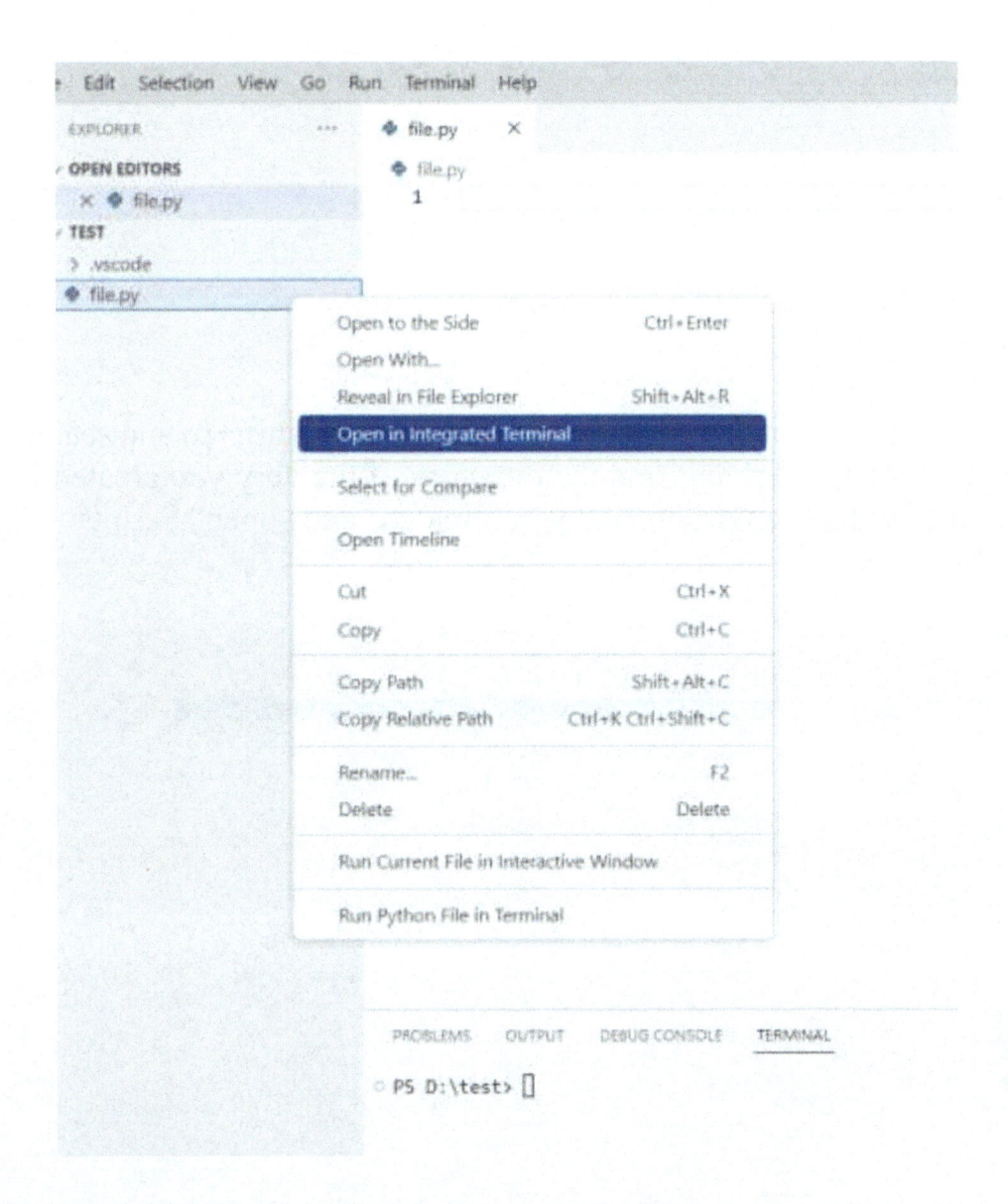

7. In the opened terminal, write `python -m venv testenv`
   NB: instead of testenv you can write whatever name you have in mind
8. Then write in the terminal: `testenv/scripts/activate.bat`

Appendix 1

```
PROBLEMS    OUTPUT    DEBUG CONSOLE    TERMINAL

● PS D:\test> python -m venv testenv
○ PS D:\test>
```

9. After a few seconds, open command pallet (ctrl+shift+p) and search for 'select python interpreter' and find the directory of the very you created in step1. Go to the virtual environment you created and open Scripts. Then select python.exe.

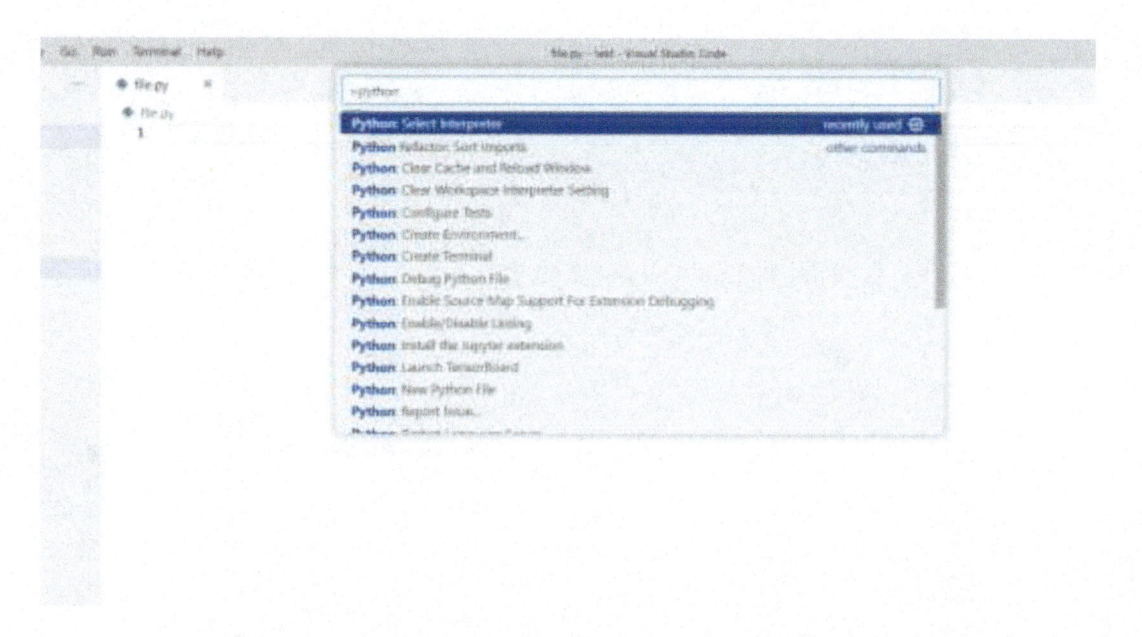

10. It is almost done. Just right click on file.py and open another terminal. If you see the following picture, the environment is ready and you can use pip to install the libraries you need.

Appendix 1

```
PS D:\test> & d:/test/testenv/Scripts/Activate.ps1
(testenv) PS D:\test>
```

Appendix 1

Appendix2

Markers for Matplotlib

Character	Description	Character	Description
'.'	Point marker	'3'	tri_left marker
','	Pixel marker	'4'	tri_right marker
'o'	Circle marker	'8'	Octagon marker
'v'	Triangle_down marker	's'	Square marker
'^'	Triangle_up marker	'p'	Pentagon marker
'<'	Triangle_left marker	'P'	Plus (filled) marker
'>'	Triangle_right marker	'*'	Star marker
'1'	tri_down marker	'h'	Hexagon1 marker
'2'	tri_up marker	'H'	Hexagon2 marker
'+'	plus marker		

Line styles for Matplotlib

Character	Description	Character	Description
'-'	solid line style	'-.'	dash-dot line style
'--'	dashed line style	':'	dotted line style

Basic Colors for Matplotlib

Character	Color	Character	Color
'b'	blue	'r'	red
'g'	green	'c'	Cyan
'm'	magenta	'k'	black
'y'	yellow	'w'	white

Printed in Great Britain
by Amazon